本书系：

江西理工大学华文教育研究中心招标课题（WYHW201501）阶段性成果

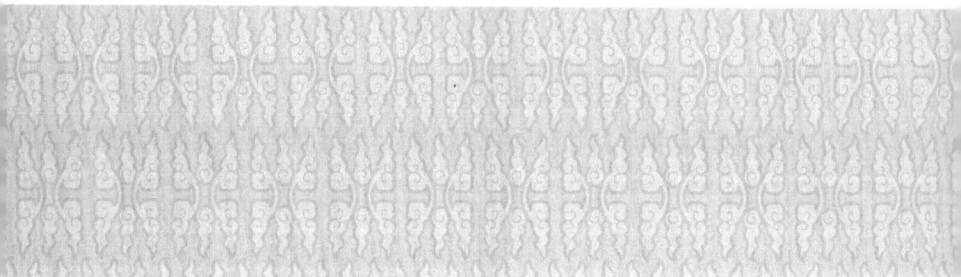

中国
经典寓言
故事

Chinese Classic Fables

李火秀　柯明星◎编著

ZHEJIANG UNIVERSITY PRESS
浙江大学出版社

总　序

海外华文教育主要是针对海外华人进行的中国语言文化教育。伴随着我国经济的快速发展、全球化进程的加快和"一带一路"倡议的提出，世界各地的华文教育，正以前所未有的速度向前推进。当前，华文教育的内容、范畴、功能、目标都从单一走向多元，华文教育教学不仅注重汉语的语音、词汇、语法、汉字等中文基础知识的讲解，而且还以弘扬中华文化、塑造中国形象、提升华人的民族文化素质与文化认同感，促进中外文化交流，增进中外友谊为重要目标。中华文化及相关内涵精神的独特魅力，通过华文教育教学，获得了海外华人以及越来越多非华裔外国人的了解、熟悉和应用，中华文化及其所蕴含的普适性价值在异域大放光彩。基于此，海外同胞把华文教育视作"留根工程"，同时也是提高后代素质，参与竞争的"希望工程"，其意义重大而深远。

I

在这一新形势下，我校（江西理工大学）始终坚持开放办学的思想，在教育国际化和华文教育工作方面取得了可喜成绩。截至目前，我校与美国、英国、法国、韩国、日本、泰国等 20 多个国家的高校和企业建立了交流与合作关系。其中，与泰国宋卡王子大学的合作交流，早在 20 多年前就已经展开，双方每年都开展多次师生互访并联合培养博士、硕士研究生。近年来，面对国内外华文教育迅猛发展的形势，我校于 2008 年创办对外汉语专业（后更名为汉语国际教育专业）；2011 年 11 月，国务院侨务办公室下发《关于同意江西理工大学建立华文教育基地的批复》的文件，使我校成为江西第二个、赣州第一个华文教育基地；2012 年 3 月，我校外语外贸学院成立了"江西理工大学华文教育研究中心"；2014 年 12 月，学校同意将研究中心升级为校级科研平台进行管理和建设；2015 年我校与巴基斯坦旁遮普大学签署共建孔子学院的协议，实现了我校在海外设立孔子学院的重大历史性突破。2017 年 6 月，教育部下发了《关于公布 2017 年

教育部国别和区域研究中心备案名单的通知》，我校申报的巴基斯坦研究中心成功获批备案。 所有这些喜人的成绩离不开我校各级领导在华文教育教学和管理工作方面的夙夜在公、殚精竭虑，离不开所有教师的恪尽职守、勤勉敬业，离不开所有与华文教育教学工作相关教师的勠力同心、砥砺奋进。 当然，我们深知中华传统文化博大精深，要将我国传统文化发扬光大，使传统文化在当代引起共鸣与认同，我们责无旁贷，任重而道远。

为此，我们编写了一套"魅力汉语·悦读经典"丛书，精选中华传统文化，文学中最经典、最有价值的神话传说、寓言故事、美德故事、戏剧故事等。 本套丛书为了便于读者能够独立阅读，在保持原著精髓的基础上，采用平实流畅、简洁生动的语言讲述故事。 每篇故事均配汉语拼音、中英文对照、故事寓意的品读，并且每篇都绘制了一幅精美插图。另外，丛书对一些生难字词做了中英文注释。 这些都可以让读者增强阅读印象，更好地领略经典名作的魅力，体验人类

最高尚的情感和最珍贵的品质，进而提升知识理解水平和审美鉴赏能力，获得心灵的滋养和精神的洗礼。

　　本套丛书不仅可以成为汉语学习者学习汉语、理解中华文化的专门读本，也可以成为英语学习者扩大阅读视野、提升英语水平的专门文本。当然，丛书中精选的内容同样可以成为广大文学爱好者品读经典，了解中国传统文化的通识读物。

Foreword

Chinese language and culture education, mainly aiming at teaching the overseas Chinese language and culture of China, is advancing at an unprecedented speed, along with the rapid economic development, accelerated globalization and proposing of the Belt and Road Initiative. Currently, the content, category, function and goal of Chinese language and culture education have developed from simplification to diversification. It not only focuses on imparting Chinese phonetics, vocabulary, grammar, and Chinese characters, but also aims to advance the Chinese culture, shape China's image in the world, improve the overseas Chinese people's national cultural awareness and identity, promote the Sino-foreign cultural exchange and strengthen the Sino-foreign friendship. Chinese culture and the charm of its connotations are understood, well-known and used by more and more overseas Chinese and non-Chinese foreigners through the Chinese language and culture education. The universal values of Chinese culture are shining brightly overseas. Besides, overseas Chinese regard the Chinese language and culture education as the "Root

V

Project" and the "Hope Project" which aims at improving the descendants' cultural accomplishment, carrying great and profound significance.

In this new situation, Jiangxi University of Science and Technology insists on the running of open education and has made great achievements on international education as well as the Chinese language and culture education. Till now, our university has set up collaborative relationships with universities and enterprises in more than 20 countries like the USA, the UK, France, R. O. Korea, Japan, Thailand, etc. The collaboration with Prince of Songkla University started over twenty years ago. Each year, many teachers and students pay exchange visits between our university and Prince of Songkla University where doctoral candidates and postgraduates have been co-cultivated. In recent years, as Chinese language and culture education has rapidly developed, our university began to recruit students majoring in Teaching Chinese as a Foreign Language in 2008 which was later renamed as Chinese International Education. In November, 2011, the Overseas Chinese Affairs Office issued the file "Approval of Jiangxi University of Science and Technology as the Chinese Language and Cultural Education Base" which enabled

us to be the second Chinese language and culture education base in Jiangxi Province and the first one in Ganzhou City. In March, 2012, a research center of Chinese language and culture education was set up in our faculty and then upgraded as a university research platform in December, 2014. Next year, a Confucius Institute was co-founded overseas by Pakistan's Punjab University and us, which was a historic breakthrough. The Pakistan Research Center in our university was in the name list reported for record as the National and Regional Research Centers approved by the Ministry of Education of China in June, 2017. All these achievements are attributed to the hard work of leaders and teachers at all levels in our university and particularly those teachers working for the Chinese language and culture education. Of course, we surely know the extensiveness and profoundness of traditional Chinese culture. Therefore, we will spare no effort to promote and develop traditional Chinese culture to gain more acceptance and resonance in the contemporary world.

For this purpose, we compiled this series named "Charming Chinese, Classic Reading", in which the most classic, valuable stories in the form of

myths, fables, virtue and drama stories about traditional Chinese culture and literature were selected. To enable readers to do the reading pleasantly, all the stories in both Chinese and English, with a vivid picture at the beginning and comment at the end, are edited with plain, concise but vivid words, going with Chinese characters and corresponding pinyin. Besides, notes are given for some difficult words. In this way, readers may have a joyful reading experience to appreciate the charm of the classics, the noblest emotions and the precious characters of humans, which in turn will help them improve their comprehension and aesthetic appreciation ability and eventually receive spiritual nourishment and baptism.

This series of stories render learners of Chinese a way to learn Chinese language and culture, broaden their reading vision and improve their English reading ability. Meanwhile, these books can be a good choice for those lovers of literature to learn traditional Chinese culture.

前　言

寓言是一种比较常用的文学体裁，它往往用短小精悍、形象生动的故事来阐述意味深长的道理，给人以启迪。中国和印度、希腊同为世界寓言文学的三大发祥地。我国寓言故事源远流长，从先秦到现在已经有两千多年的发展历史。它不仅对中国文化，而且对世界文化有着极其深远的影响。它是世界文学艺术百花园里的奇葩，是人类艺术宝库中的块宝。

我国寓言博大精深，彰显了中华民族精神和各个历史时代的特色，它的显著特点是：

第一，一般采用故事与寓意相结合的形式，通过故事来阐明道理，或是寄托某种讽刺或劝诫的含义。如《东郭先生和狼》通过东郭先生救助一匹狼的故事，揭示了我们对坏人要保持警惕性，不要向坏人滥施同情的道理；《无价之宝》叙述人们对珍奇珠宝竞相追逐的故事，告诫人们只有美德才是无价的宝贝；《覆车之鉴》则告诉我们为人处世不要妄自尊大，

而应该谦虚谨慎。所有的这些寓言，都是旨在让人在聆听故事的同时，去领会、思考作者要讲的道理，劝善惩恶，给人以警醒。

第二，常用的艺术手法是拟人化和夸张。作者往往将自然界中动、植物的形象人格化，使它们具有人的思想情感、语言和行动。而且，作者会运用大胆的想象、夸张或渲染等艺术手法，使自己讲述的故事更为突出鲜明，给读者以奇特、强烈乃至震撼的感受，从而启发人们更为深刻地认清事物的本质。在作者笔下，飞禽走兽、花草树木，均被赋予灵性和智慧。如《狐假虎威》《井底之蛙》《寒号鸟》《向日葵和石头》等，都是以动物或植物等自然界物种为主人公，通过它们的视角，对现实社会的各种现象做深刻的揭露。

第三，故事语言呈现出精练、简明、朴实、生动的特点。作者主要是通过简明扼要、通俗易懂的故事来阐发道理。所以，为了能够更好理解、领会其中的奥妙与哲理，寓言

一般不采用华丽、典雅或是其他修饰性的词语。 如《活到老学到老》《人穷志不短》《书呆子赶鸡》《秀才的"大志"》等故事，通过明白流畅的语言，讲述了一个个形象生动的故事，使读者很容易就明白其中蕴含的道理。

我国古代寓言故事题材来源于现实生活，是人们集体智慧的结晶。 生动有趣的小故事，凝聚着智者对于社会万象、人生百态的思考，故事中蕴含了警世醒人的大智慧。 总之，阅读它们，我们可以学到许多生活哲理，学会明辨是非，知晓民族大义，懂得自省与自律，并能够对我们的学习和生活有所助益。

《中国经典寓言故事》从我国浩如烟海的寓言王国里，精心挑选了 55 篇寓意深刻的经典寓言故事，按照哲理、劝诫、讽刺、诙谐四大类别进行编排。 本书采用故事加注拼音与中英文对照、生难字词中英文注释的方式，以精练的语言讲述故事，并根据情节配以精美的插图。 为了帮助读者理解

作品，我们在每篇寓言后面都配上了故事寓意，希望能给读者一点点启发。

　　品读寓言经典，构织精彩人生，让生命在阅读中得到升华，让人生在阅读中更加充实。

编者

2016 年 1 月 5 日

Preface

Fable is a literary genre in which short stories are used to expose a truth or moral lesson to its readers. China, India and Greece are the three major birthplaces of fable. It has a long history in China, being known from before the Qin dynasty over 2,000 years ago. Fables have had profound influence not only on Chinese culture and history, but also on civilizations all around the world. They are the stunning flowers in the garden of literature and rare gems in the treasure house of art.

Fables have demonstrated the national spirit and characteristics of China during different periods. There are several noticeable features in these fable stores.

Firstly, thematically, they generally concern morality and truth and their nature is often satirical. For instance, "Mr. Dongguo and the Wolf", in which the eponym rescues a wolf only to be menaced by it, cautions vigilance against those we don't know, and to refrain from helping them blindly. In "The Invaluable Treasure" Longmenzi teaches us to value a healthy mind and benevolent heart over exotic but meaningless material

goods. "The Lesson of an Overturned Carriage" advocates modesty and prudence through the wisdom of a teacher during a rainy walk with his students. All these fables are written so that the reader might grasp and ponder upon their author's message, and the warnings therein.

Secondly, personification and hyperbole are commonly used in Chinese fables. Their authors often endow animals and plants with thought, emotion, language and actions like those of mankind. They are imaginatively rich, so as to inspire the reader to get a thorough understanding of their essence. Animals, flowers and trees are endowed with intelligence and wisdom and shaped as leading characters, as in "The Fox Assuming the Majesty of the Tiger", "The Frog at the Bottom of a Well", "The Hanhao Bird", "The Sunflower and the Stone" Various kinds of phenomena in society are exposed through these figures.

Thirdly, the language in fables is refined, concise and vivid. The stories are pithy and easy-to-read. They generally avoid elaborate or convoluted vocabulary so that the reader might better understand the message.

Through clear and lucid language, fables such as "Live and Learn", "Poor but With Lofty Ideals", "The Bookworm Shooing the Chickens", "The Scholars' Ambition" and so on all tell vivid stories whose truths are easily understood by readers.

Chinese ancient fables stem from real life, and they are the accumulation of people's wisdom. These tales reflect on all kinds of phenomena of society and life in evocative and interesting stories which contain enlightening wisdom to awaken people. Reading them can help us acquire life philosophy, distinguish right from wrong and come to know more about our national spirit and character. We can learn to self-examine and self-control, which are beneficial to our study and life.

In *Chinese Classic Fables* , 55 stories are chosen from countless classical texts, according to the four categories of philosophy, exhortation, irony and humour. Stories in the English version are combined with the Chinese version and pinyin. Also included are glossaries of difficult words both in English and Chinese. The fables are told in a succinct way,

and illustrated with beautiful pictures accordingly. In order to inspire and to help the reader comprehend their meaning, the moral of each tale is included.

Let us read classic fables and enrich our lives. Reading makes our lives sublime and colourful.

Compilers

January 5, 2016

目　录
Contents

第三辑
Part 3

中

国

经

典

寓

言

故

事

第一辑

Part 1

不受嗟来之食

Not to Accept Food Handed Out in Contempt

zhàn guó shí qī zhū hóu guó zhī jiān jīng cháng fā shēng zhàn zhēng lǎo
战国时期，诸侯国之间经常发生战争。老

bǎi xìng shēng huó zài shuǐ shēn huǒ rè zhī zhōng shēng huó shí fēn jiān kǔ jiǎ
百姓生活在水深火热之中，生活十分艰苦。假

ruò yù dào zāi huāng lǎo bǎi xìng de rì zi gèng jiā méi fǎr guò le
若遇到灾荒，老百姓的日子更加没法儿过了。

yǒu yì nián qí guó fā shēng hàn zāi zhěng zhěng sān gè duō yuè bù
有一年，齐国发生旱灾，整整三个多月不

céng jiàng yì dī yǔ tián dì kāi liè zhuāng jia quán dōu bèi shài sǐ le
曾降一滴雨。田地开裂，庄稼全都被晒死了。

qióng kǔ rén jiā méi yǒu liáng shi chī zhǐ děi qù chī shù yè shù pí chī cǎo
穷苦人家没有粮食吃，只得去吃树叶、树皮，吃草

gēn jiù suàn shì zhè yàng hái shì yǒu hěn duō rén bèi è sǐ le kě shì
根。就算是这样，还是有很多人被饿死了。可是，

那些有钱人的家里，粮食堆满仓库，不愁吃穿。

有一个富人名叫黔敖，他看到穷人们的痛苦，心里十分得意。他想自己无论如何也不会落到如此境地。他想拿出点粮食分发给穷人，但又摆出一副救世主的架子。他把做好的馒头摆在路边，施舍给路过的穷人。每当过来一个饥饿的人，黔敖就丢一个馒头过去，并且傲慢地说道："讨饭的，给你吃吧！"有时候，过来一群人，黔敖便丢出去好几个馒头让大家互相争抢，自己则在一旁看热闹，他觉得自己很了不起。

这时，走过来一个饿得不成样子的人。他衣衫破烂，头发乱蓬蓬的。由于好几天都没吃东西了，他连路都走不稳，摇摇晃晃地，好像要晕倒一样。黔敖看见这个人，便拿了两个馒头，还

tè yì yǎo le yì wǎn tāng　dà shēng yāo he zhe　　wèi　guò lái chī　　kě
特意舀了一碗汤，大声吆喝着："喂，过来吃！"可

shì　nà ge rén hǎo xiàng méi yǒu tīng jiàn yí yàng　méi yǒu lǐ tā　qián áo
是，那个人好像没有听见一样，没有理他。黔敖

yòu jiào dào　tīng dào méi yǒu　jiào nǐ ne　gěi nǐ chī de　zhǐ jiàn nà
又叫道："听到没有？叫你呢，给你吃的！"只见那

ge rén tái qǐ tóu　dèng dà shuāng yǎn　kàn zhe qián áo shuō　shōu qǐ nǐ
个人抬起头，瞪大双眼，看着黔敖说："收起你

de shí wù ba　wǒ nìng yuàn è　sǐ yě bú yuàn chī zhè yàng de jiē lái zhī
的食物吧，我宁愿饿死也不愿吃这样的嗟来之

shí　qián áo tīng le hěn cán kuì　hòu lái qián áo xiàng nà ge rén péi lǐ
食！"黔敖听了很惭愧。后来黔敖向那个人赔礼

dào qiàn　dàn nà ge rén hái shì bù kěn chī tā de shí wù　zuì hòu è sǐ zài
道歉，但那个人还是不肯吃他的食物，最后饿死在

le lù biān
了路边。

During the Warring States period, the vassal states always
fought against each other, and people lived with great suffering.
Natural disasters made it even harder to survive.

One year, the State of Qi was burdened wit drought for 3
successive months. The land cracked and all the crops were burnt.
The poor people had nothing to eat, and they had to eat the
leaves, barks and grassroots. Even in this way, still many people
starved to death. Meanwhile, the rich folk didn't need to worry

because their barns were heaped up with crops.

A rich man named Qian Ao took pleasure in others' misfortune and thought that he would never fall into such a terrible situation. He decided to send some food to the poor, but he acted as if he was the savior.

He placed buns at one side of the road and distributed them to the poor people passing by. Once a hungry man came over, he would throw a bun to him and called arrogantly, "Beggar, eat this." Sometimes, when a group of people came, he would throw several buns for them to fight and catch, and then he stood by to laugh at them, regarding himself as a living Buddha with great kindness.

Then, there came a bony man with shabby clothes and matted hair. The man couldn't even walk for he hadn't eaten anything for several days. He staggered and was about to fall down. Seeing this man, Qian Ao took two buns and filled a bowl of soup, shouting, "Come and eat." But the man ignored Qian Ao as if he did not hear the words. Qian Ao yelled again, "Did you hear me? Hey, you, here is the food." Then the man raised his head and stared at him, "Pack up your things. I would rather starve to death than take such handout." Qian Ao felt embarrassed and apologized to the man. But the man still didn't accept his food and eventually died of hunger beside the road.

生难字/词注解 | Notes

诸侯国：中文狭义上指中国历史上秦朝以前分封制下，中原王朝的最高统治者天子对封地的称呼。

Vassal states：It refers to the feudal states before the Qin Dynasty in China.

嗟：不礼貌的招呼声，相当于现在的喂、嘿。

Jie：A mimetic word，a greeting that is not polite such as "hey" and "well".

故事寓意 | The moral of the story

"嗟来之食"形容带有侮辱性或不怀好意的施舍。"不受嗟来之食"是指绝不低三下四地接受别人的施舍。这个故事告诉我们：对他人应该心存善意，不应该以"救世主"的姿态凌驾于他人之上。只有真心诚意地帮助别人，我们才能体会到帮助别人所带来的乐趣。

"Food handed out in contempt" is used to describe charity with insult or malicious intention. "Not to accept food handed out in contempt" means that people refuse to accept others' charity without sincerity. The story tells us that we should treat others with good intention instead of feeling superior to others. Only when we help others sincerely, can we feel the pleasure of helping others.

曹冲称象

Cao Chong Weighing the Elephant

sān guó shí qī　wèi wáng cáo cāo zuì xiǎo de ér zi　míng jiào cáo
三国时期，魏王曹操最小的儿子，名叫曹

chōng　cáo chōng hěn xiǎo de shí hou jiù fēi cháng cōng míng　xǐ huān sī kǎo
冲。曹冲很小的时候就非常聪明，喜欢思考。

zhǐ yǒu wǔ liù suì de nián jì　jiù kě yǐ xiǎng chū hěn duō bàn fǎ lái jiě jué
只有五六岁的年纪，就可以想出很多办法来解决

wèn tí
问题。

yǒu yí cì　wú wáng sūn quán pài rén gěi cáo cāo sòng lái le　yì tóu dà
有一次，吴王孙权派人给曹操送来了一头大

xiàng zuò wéi lǐ wù　cáo cāo dì yī cì kàn jiàn zhè yàng páng dà de dòng
象作为礼物。曹操第一次看见这样庞大的动

wù　shí fēn hào qí　tā wèn sòng dà xiàng lái de rén　zhè tóu dà xiàng
物，十分好奇。他问送大象来的人："这头大象

jiū jìng yǒu duō zhòng ne　lái rén huí dá　wǒ men cóng lái méi yǒu chēng guò
究竟有多重呢？"来人回答："我们从来没有称过

dà xiàng　bù zhī dào dà xiàng yǒu duō zhòng　qǐng nín xiǎng gè bàn fǎ chēng
大象，不知道大象有多重。请您想个办法称

chēng dà xiàng de zhòng liàng ba
称大象的重量吧。"

yú shì cáo cāo zhào jí dà chén shuō néng chēng chū dà xiàng zhòng
于是，曹操召集大臣，说："能称出大象重

liàng de rén huì dé dào fēng hòu de shǎng cì dà jiā dōu hěn jī jí de
量的人，会得到丰厚的赏赐。"大家都很积极地

xiǎng bàn fǎ yǒu rén shuō yào zuò yì gǎn dà chèng cáo cāo fǎn bó shuō jiù shì
想办法，有人说要做一杆大秤，曹操反驳说就是

zuò chū lái le yě méi yǒu rén néng tí de qǐ lái chēng a yǒu rén shuō yào
做出来了，也没有人能提得起来称啊；有人说要

bǎ dà xiàng jù chéng xiǎo kuài lái chēng cáo cāo zhǐ zé shuō bù kě yǐ bǎ lǐ
把大象锯成小块来称，曹操指责说不可以把礼

wù huǐ huài
物毁坏。

jiù zài dà jiā kǔ kǔ sī kǎo de shí hou xiǎo cáo chōng hū rán zǒu dào
就在大家苦苦思考的时候，小曹冲忽然走到

cáo cāo shēn biān shuō dào fù wáng bié zháo jí wǒ yǒu bàn fǎ wǒ men kě
曹操身边说道："父王别着急，我有办法，我们可

yǐ xiān bǎ dà xiàng qiān dào chuán shang zài chuán bāng qí shuǐ chù zuò gè jì
以先把大象牵到船上，在船帮齐水处做个记

hao rán hòu bǎ dà xiàng qiān zǒu zài bǎ shí tou yùn dào chuán shang yì zhí
号。然后把大象牵走，再把石头运到船上，一直

dào chuán shēn xià jiàng dào xiān qián zuò de jì hao wéi zhǐ zhè shí shí tou de
到船身下降到先前做的记号为止，这时石头的

zhòng liàng jiù hé dà xiàng de zhòng liàng xiāng děng le rán hòu wǒ men zài
重量就和大象的重量相等了。然后，我们再

bǎ shí tou fēn bié chēng yi chēng bǎ zhè xiē zhòng liàng jiā qǐ lái jiù zhī
把石头分别称一称，把这些重量加起来，就知

dào dà xiàng yǒu duō zhòng le àn zhào cáo chōng de bàn fǎ dà xiàng de
道大象有多重了。"按照曹冲的办法，大象的

zhòng liàng zhōng yú bèi chēng chū lái le   cáo cāo fēi cháng gāo xìng   dà jiā dōu
重 量 终 于 被 称 出 来 了，曹 操 非 常 高 兴，大 家 都

chēng zàn cáo chōng de cōng míng
称 赞 曹 冲 的 聪 明。

During the Three Kingdoms period, the youngest son of Cao Cao was named Cao Chong. Ever since Cao Chong was a kid, he was very smart and could come up with many good ideas when he was only five or six years old.

Once, the Emperor of the State of Wu, Sun Quan sent an elephant as a gift to Cao Cao. Cao Cao was very curious to see such a huge animal for the first time, so he asked the person who came to deliver the elephant, "How much does the elephant weigh?" "We have never weighed an elephant, so we don't know. Can you please find a way to weigh the elephant?" the man replied.

Then Cao Cao summoned all the ministers and said that whoever can think of a way to weigh the elephant would get rewarded. Everybody tried hard to find a good way. Someone suggested to make a large steelyard but Cao Cao refuted that no one could put it up even if it could be made. Another person said that they could cut the elephant into small pieces, but Cao Cao criticized that it would kill the gift.

When all of them were racking their wits, Cao Chong went to Cao Cao and said, "Don't worry, father. I have one idea. First, we lead the elephant to a boat，and mark the water line where the water comes up. Then we lead the elephant away and put the heavy stones in the boat until the water comes up to the same line. Thus，the weight of the elephant equals that of the stones. Then we just need to weigh the stones bit by bit and add them up，and we could know the weight of the elephant." According to Cao Chong's approach，they finally found out the weight of the elephant. Cao Cao was very happy，and all the people praised Cao Chong for his wisdom.

生难字/词注解 | Note

秤：衡量轻重的器具。
Steelyard：A measure tool of weight.

故事寓意 | The moral of the story

曹冲年纪虽小,却有超越一般人的智慧。这个故事告诉我们：在生活中要善于观察,逾越常规性思维,去思考、解决问题。

As a little kid，Cao Chong was full of extraordinary wisdom. This story tells us that in our life, we should try to solve problems by observing carefully and thinking out of the box.

飞蛾投火

The Moth Darting into the Flame

yì tiān yǒu yí hù rén jiā lái le kè rén   wǎn shang dà jiā zuò
一天，有一户人家来了客人。晚上，大家坐

zài yuàn zi lǐ xián liáo shí fēn kāi xīn   zhōu wéi shí fēn yōu jìng zhǐ yǒu yì
在院子里闲聊，十分开心。周围十分幽静，只有一

zhī là zhú zài bù yuǎn chù shǎn zhe wēi guāng   là zhú de guāng liàng zài hēi
支蜡烛在不远处闪着微光。蜡烛的光亮在黑

yè lǐ xiǎn de gé wài de yào yǎn
夜里显得格外的耀眼。

zhè shí   yì zhī fēi é pū dǎ zhe chì bǎng   bù tíng de rào zhe zhú
这时，一只飞蛾扑打着翅膀，不停地绕着烛

guāng fēi lái fēi qù   hái fā chū xì xiǎo de sī sī shēng   zhè shēng yīn dǎ
光飞来飞去，还发出细小的嘶嘶声，这声音打

rǎo le tán huà rén de xìng zhì   zhǔ rén biàn yòng shàn zi qū gǎn fēi é   fēi
扰了谈话人的兴致。主人便用扇子驱赶飞蛾，飞

蛾看见有人赶它,便飞走了。可是,不一会儿它又飞回来了,主人又去赶它,可是它才飞走不久便又飞回来了,还不顾一切地,一个劲儿地朝烛火扑过去。如此反反复复了七八次,不管你怎么驱赶,它都会回来。终于,飞蛾的翅膀被烛火烧焦了,它再也飞不动了,落到了地上。可都这样了它还是不甘心,它仍旧不停地扑动着那已经被烤得残破的翅膀,直到耗尽最后一丝气息。

看了这一凄惨的场景,主人十分感慨,说:"飞蛾扑火多么愚蠢啊!明知道会引火烧身,结束自己的生命,还偏要不顾一切地扑过去,结果落得这样的下场!"客人也感叹道:"是呀,人有时候也有执念,就像飞蛾一样,明知会走向毁灭,却仍然不顾一切地去争夺追逐,最后落得个悲惨的下场!这真是令人可悲可叹呀!"

One day, a family was entertaining a guest and in the evening they all sat in the yard, chatting and having a great time. It was quiet and calm around them with only a candle dimly lit not far away. The light of the candle looked extraordinarily dazzling in the night.

At that moment, a moth fluttered and kept flying around the light, making a low hiss. This sound disturbed them a lot, so the master expelled it with his fan. The moth flew away but soon it flew back. The master then again tried to drive it away, but it just returned soon after it flew away. It flew all the way to the flame desperately. It happened for about 7 or 8 times, and no matter how the master expelled it, it would come back all the time. Finally, the moth's wings were charred by the flame and it couldn't move anymore and fell to the ground. Though, it still refused to be defeated, beating its wings which had already been burnt into broken pieces till its last breath.

After seeing this pathetic scene, the master sighed and said, "How stupid the moth is! In spite of knowing that the flame would burn itself and end its life, the moth still insisted on darting into the flame." The guest also exclaimed, "Yeah, sometimes people act just like the moth, knowing that it would ruin itself but still fight desperately for it and finally end up with a tragedy. How deplorable it is."

故事寓意 | The moral of the story

　　"飞蛾投火",常用来比喻自寻死路、自取灭亡。后来引申为为了某一个既定目标而不顾一切地去努力奋斗。这个故事告诫我们做事要有法度、规则,要有张有弛,这样才能生活得充实自在,不致毁灭了自我。

　　"The moth darting into the flame" is used to describe people who would head to their doom. It is interpreted as someone desperately striving for his goals. The story warns us that we should work with norms and rules, and be flexible. Only in this way can we lead a rich and comfortable life, and not go so far as to destroy ourselves.

后来居上

Newcomers Come to the Fore

hàn wǔ dì shí qī   huáng dì shēn biān yǒu sān wèi zhù míng de dà chén
汉武帝时期，皇帝身边有三位著名的大臣，

fēn bié shì jí àn gōng sūn hóng hé zhāng tāng   sān rén suī rán tóng shí zài
分别是汲黯、公孙弘和张汤。三人虽然同时在

cháo tíng zuò guān dàn tā men de zī lì què hěn bù yí yàng   jí àn dào
朝廷做官，但他们的资历却很不一样。汲黯到

gōng lǐ gōng zuò de shí hou zī lì yǐ jīng hěn shēn le guān wèi yě hěn gāo
宫里工作的时候，资历已经很深了，官位也很高。

ér gōng sūn hóng hé zhāng tāng liǎng rén dōu hái zhǐ shì guān wèi bēi xià de xiǎo
而公孙弘和张汤两人都还只是官位卑下的小

guān lì   chù chù shòu rén diāo nàn   bú guò zhí wèi dī bú dài biǎo néng lì bù
官吏，处处受人刁难。不过职位低不代表能力不

zú gōng sūn hóng hé zhāng tāng píng shí dài rén jiē wù hé shàn qiān xùn   shēn
足，公孙弘和张汤平时待人接物和善谦逊，深

得汉武帝的喜爱。后来他们两人都得到了皇帝

的重用和提拔，公孙弘位至宰相，张汤也升

任为御史大夫，两人的官职都排在了汲黯前面。

汲黯的政绩一般，平时为人傲慢。他看到公孙

弘和张汤这两个后来之辈受到了提拔，官位竟

在他之上，心里很不是滋味，总想找个机会让

皇帝评评这个理。

有一天，汉武帝和大臣们讨论完公事后，正

准备去散步。这时汲黯赶紧走到了皇帝面前，

说："皇上，臣有句话想禀报您，不知您是否感

兴趣？"汉武帝好奇地问道："是什么事啊？说来

听听。"汲黯说："皇上您见过农夫堆积柴草吗？

他们总是把先搬来的柴草铺在底层，后来搬来的

反而放在上面，您不觉得那些先搬来的柴草太委

屈了吗？"汉武帝很疑惑，不知道汲黯到底想表达

什么意思。汲黯接着说："公孙弘、张汤那些小官，论资历、职位都在我之下，可现在他们却后来者居上，职位都比我高了许多。皇上您这样做，不是跟那堆放柴草的农夫一样吗？"汉武帝听了，心里很不高兴。他觉得汲黯这人不通情理，而且分析问题简单、片面。

从那以后，汉武帝不再重视汲黯，汲黯再也没有升过职。

During the period of Emperor Wu of the Han Dynasty, the Emperor had three famous ministers, namely Ji An, Gongsun Hong and Zhang Tang. Although the three were all officials served in the court at the same time, their qualifications were quite different. When Ji An came to the court, he was in a high position with rich experience. However Gongsun Hong and Zhang Tang were still at low positions and always encountered a lot of troubles. But low official position does not mean low ability. Gongsun Hong and Zhang Tang were kind and generous, humble and gentle, thus they won the favor of Emperor Wu. Both of them later were promoted by the Emperor, with Gongsun Hong promoted to the position of chief chancellor, and Zhang Tang promoted as grand censor. The official positions of the two people were ranked in front of Ji An's. But Ji An was very arrogant in daily life and he was not outstanding in his official career. Seeing Gongsun Hong and Zhang Tang as two newcomers surpassed him, he was unpleasant and always want to find an opportunity to ask the Emperor to judge.

One day, after finishing the consulting of the affairs of state with chancellors, Emperor Wu was ready to go for a walk. Just at that moment, Ji An quickly went to the Emperor and said, "Emperor, I want to report something to you, and I wonder if you are interested in that." The Emperor asked curiously, "Oh, what is going on? Tell me." Ji An answered, "Emperor, have you ever seen how farmers pile up the straw? They always put the straw which they bring earlier in the lower level and the straw they bring later in the upper. Do not you think the straw at the bottom may feel wronged?" The Emperor felt confused about what Ji An wanted to express. Then Ji An said, "Gongsun Hong and Zhang Tang were of low status, and they were far behind me in terms of experience and positions. But now, the newcomers are in the front, and their positions are even higher than me. Emperor, isn't it just the same as the farmer putting the first-arrived straw at the bottom?" Hearing that, the Emperor felt annoyed and regarded Ji An as an unreasonable person who always focused on one-side of a problem.

Ever since then, the Emperor no longer appreciated Ji An, and Ji An never got promoted.

生难字/词注解 | Notes

宰相：中国古代最高行政长官的通称。

Chancellor：The common appellation of ancient China's chief administrative officials.

御史大夫：官名，秦代始置，负责监察百官，代表皇帝接受百官奏事，管理国家重要图册、典籍，代朝廷起草诏命文书等。

Grand censor：The title of an official position which is initially set in the Qin Dynasty to take charge of supervising all the officers, listening to the reports of the officers, managing the important albums and precious books of the country, making drafts of government documents.

故事寓意 | The moral of the story

"后来居上"，用来形容后来者可以胜过排在前面位置的人。汉武帝用人唯贤，而汲黯认为提拔人才一定要论资排辈。汲黯心胸狭窄，目光短浅，以至于被汉武帝冷落。这个故事告诉我们：要戒骄戒躁，不断地提升自己的学识，增强才干，这样才不会落后于人。

"Newcomers come to the fore" is used to describe that the newcomers can surpass others who are senior to them. Emperor Wu of the Han Dynasty chose officials for positions according to their ability, but Ji An thought that promotion must be

arranged in order of seniority. Ji An was narrow-minded and shortsighted, so he was left out by Emperor Wu. This story tells us that we should abstain from arrogance and anxiety, improve our knowledge gradually and enhance our ability, so as not to lag behind others.

活到老学到老

Live and Learn

jìn píng gōng shì yì guó de huáng dì　tā zhì guó yǒu fāng　zhèng jì
晋平公是一国的皇帝，他治国有方，政绩

xiǎn zhù　tā zǒng jué de zì jǐ xué shí cū qiǎn　xī wàng néng gòu duō dú
显著。他总觉得自己学识粗浅，希望能够多读

diǎn shū　zēng zhǎng jiàn shi　kāi tuò yǎn jiè　kě shì　jìn píng gōng yòu hěn
点书，增长见识，开拓眼界。可是，晋平公又很

huái yí zì jǐ de xué xí néng lì　tā xiǎng　wǒ dōu yǐ jīng qī shí suì
怀疑自己的学习能力。他想：我都已经七十岁

le　nà me dà de nián jì le　xiàn zài qù xué xí　kěn dìng shì fēi cháng kùn
了，那么大的年纪了，现在去学习，肯定是非常困

nan de　xué hái shì bù xué　zhè ràng jìn píng gōng hěn kǔ nǎo　wèi le jiě
难的。学还是不学，这让晋平公很苦恼。为了解

jué zhè ge wèn tí　tā jué dìng qù xún wèn gōng zhōng de dà chén shī kuàng
决这个问题，他决定去询问宫中的大臣师旷。

师旷是一位双目失明的老人,他学识渊博,很有智慧。虽然他的眼睛看不见,但是却能将世事看得很通透。晋平公问师旷说:"我已经七十岁了,可是我希望还能够多读些书,增长自己的学问。可是我又总是没有信心,觉得现在学习好像太晚了点儿。"师旷回答说:"您说太晚了,为什么不把蜡烛点起来呢?"晋平公听了很不高兴,觉得师旷在戏弄他。

师旷连忙解释道:"皇上,我是您的臣子,怎么敢戏弄大王呢?我是在认真地跟您谈学习的事呢!"师旷接着说:"我听说人在少年时期学习,就如同早晨温暖的阳光一样,那太阳越照越亮,时间也持续很久。人在壮年的时候学习,就好比中午明亮的阳光一样,虽然中午的太阳已走了一半了,可它依旧很有力量,时间也还有

xǔ duō　　rén dào lǎo nián de shí hou xué xí　　jiù rú　yǐ luò shān de tài yáng
许多。人到老年的时候学习，就如已落山的太阳，

suī rán méi yǒu le guāng liàng　　kě shì tā hái kě yǐ jiè zhù là zhú de guāng
虽然没有了光亮，可是它还可以借助蜡烛的光

máng a　　suī rán là zhú de guāng liàng shí fēn wēi ruò　　dàn zǒng bǐ zài hēi
芒啊。虽然蜡烛的光亮十分微弱，但总比在黑

àn zhōng jiān nán mō suǒ yào hǎo duō le ba
暗中艰难摸索要好多了吧。"

jìn píng gōng tīng hòu　　huǎng rán dà wù　　tā gāo xìng de shuō　　nǐ shuō
晋平公听后，恍然大悟，他高兴地说："你说

de tài hǎo le　　wǒ xiàn zài zhī dào gāi zěn me zuò le
得太好了，我现在知道该怎么做了。"

Duke Ping of the State of Jin was tactful in governing his country and he had made prominent achievements. But he always thought himself lacking in knowledge and was thirsty to read more books to expand his knowledge and broaden his view. However, he always had a suspicion of his own learning ability. He wondered, "I'm already 70 years old, and it must be very hard for me to learn at such an old age." To learn or not, this problem bothered him very much. Therefore, in order to solve the problem he made a decision that he would go to enquire of Shi Kuang, a minister in the palace.

Shi Kuang, an old blind man, was knowledgeable and wise.

The man, though blind, had a thorough understanding of the world. Duke Ping asked him, "I'm over 70, but I still hope that I can expand my knowledge by doing more reading. However, I have no confidence in it. And I'm afraid that it is too late for me to study." Shi Kuang replied, "You said it was too late to study, then why don't you light a candle?" Duke Ping felt unpleasant about the reply because he thought Shi Kuang was just making fun of him.

Shi Kuang explained in a hurry, "Emperor, I'm your minister. How dare I play tricks on you? I'm seriously talking about learning with you." Then he continued, "I heard that study during a young age is just like the warm sunshine in the early morning, and it becomes increasingly brighter and lasts for a long period of time. Study during the middle age is exactly the same as the bright sunshine at noon. Although the sun has run a half way, it is still quite powerful and has much time left. When people become old, their study is similar to the setting sun. Despite that the light is fading, we still can borrow the light from candles. Although the light of candles is very weak, it's much better than searching in the darkness."

Duke Ping was suddenly enlightened after hearing Shi Kuang's words and said excitedly, "Wonderful! Now I'm clear about what to do."

故事寓意 | The moral of the story

这个故事告诉我们：知识是无穷无尽的，人的一生就是在不断学习,不断进步。中国有句谚语,即"生命不息,学习不止"。这句话启迪我们不论年龄大小,只有坚持不懈地学习,才能通达事理,明白生命的意义与人生的真谛。

This story tells us that knowledge is illimitable, and we should keep learning and making progress during our life. There is a saying in Chinese, "As long as you're alive, keep learning." This sentence informs us that we should be persistent in studying so as to understand the rules of the world and the real meaning of life.

寒号鸟

The Hanhao Bird

chuán shuō yǒu yì zhǒng xiǎo niǎo　míng jiào hán háo niǎo　zhè zhǒng niǎo
传说有一种小鸟，名叫寒号鸟。这种鸟

yǔ qí tā niǎo bù tóng　tā zhǎng zhe sì zhī jiǎo　liǎng zhī guāng tū tū de
与其他鸟不同，它长着四只脚，两只光秃秃的

ròu chì bǎng　bù huì xiàng yì bān de niǎo nà yàng fēi xiáng　xià tiān de shí
肉翅膀，不会像一般的鸟那样飞翔。夏天的时

hou　hán háo niǎo quán shēn cháng mǎn le xuàn lì de yǔ máo　yàng zi hěn měi
候，寒号鸟全身长满了绚丽的羽毛，样子很美

lì　hán háo niǎo wèi cǐ shí fēn jiāo ào　jué de zì jǐ shì tiān dǐ xia zuì
丽。寒号鸟为此十分骄傲，觉得自己是天底下最

piào liang de niǎo le
漂亮的鸟了。

xià tiān guò qù le　qiū tiān dào le　niǎo ér men dōu fēi cháng máng lù
夏天过去了，秋天到了，鸟儿们都非常忙碌。

tā men zài zhǔn bèi zhe rú hé dù guò yán hán de dōng tiān　tā men yǒu de kāi
它们在准备着如何度过严寒的冬天。它们有的开

27

始结伴飞到南边，因为南方更加温暖；有的留在北边，就整天忙着囤积食物，修理窝巢，做好过冬的准备。只有寒号鸟，既没有飞到南方去的本领，又不愿辛勤劳动，只知道到处炫耀身上漂亮的羽毛。

冬天很快来了，天气异常寒冷，小鸟们都到自己温暖的窝巢里。这时的寒号鸟，身上漂亮的羽毛都掉落光了，白天它趁着太阳光照的热气，还能够勉强度过一天。到了晚上，它躲在石缝里，冻得浑身直打哆嗦，它不停地叫着："哆罗罗，哆罗罗，寒风冻死我呀，明天就垒窝啊！"可是，等到天亮，太阳出来了，寒号鸟忘记了夜晚的寒冷，又不愿去建造窝啦。寒号鸟就这样一天天地瞎混着，一直没有给自己垒个暖和的窝。最后，它没能度过寒冷的冬天，被冻死在岩石缝里了。

There was a legendary bird called Hanhao Bird which was different from other birds. It had four legs, two wings of bare flesh, and couldn't fly as common birds. In summer, Hanhao Bird's body was covered with bright feathers and looked very beautiful. So Hanhao Bird was incredibly proud to think itself the most beautiful bird in the world. When summer passed and autumn arrived, all the other birds were busy preparing for the cold winter. Some birds flew together to the south, getting ready to spend a warm winter there. Others who stayed in the north would hoard food and repair nests for the winter. Only Hanhao Bird who neither had the ability to fly to the south nor would like to work hard, still showed off its beautiful feathers everywhere.

The winter finally came, and the days were extremely cold. The other birds were all in their warm nests, but Hanhao Bird who had shed all its beautiful feathers just warmed itself in the sunshine. At night, it hid in a crevice, shivering and crying, "Cold, ah, ah cold. I will build a nest tomorrow!"

But when the sun came out, Hanhao Bird again forgot the coldness in the night and didn't want to build a nest. So day by day, Hanhao Bird just idled away and didn't make itself a warm nest. Finally, it could not make it through the cold winter, and eventually was frozen to death in the crevice of the rocks.

🔲 生难字/词注解 | Notes

炫耀：从某个方面特意强调、突出自己。

Show off(oneself)：Emphasize oneself from a certain aspect.

垒：用砖石木料等加以重叠堆砌起来。

Build：Make something by piling up bricks，stones.

故事寓意 | The moral of the story

这个故事告诉我们：不能只顾眼前享乐，得过且过，要依靠我们自己的辛勤劳动去创造美好幸福的生活。

This story tells us that we should not just enjoy the moment and muddle along. We should try to build a happy life through hard work.

惊弓之鸟

A Bird Startled by the Twang of a Bowstring

zhàn guó shí hou　　wèi guó yǒu yí gè zhù míng de shè jiàn néng shǒu　míng jiào
战国时候，魏国有一个著名的射箭能手，名叫

gēng léi　　　yì tiān　gēng léi yǔ wèi wáng zhàn zài yí gè gāo tái shang　tái tóu
更嬴。一天，更嬴与魏王站在一个高台上，抬头

kàn jiàn yǒu niǎo zài tiān kōng zhōng fēi　　gēng léi duì wèi wáng shuō　　qǐng dà wáng
看见有鸟在天空中飞。更嬴对魏王说："请大王

kàn kan　wǒ kě yǐ zhǐ lā gōng bù fā jiàn ér bǎ niǎo shè xià lái　　wèi wáng bù
看看，我可以只拉弓不发箭而把鸟射下来。"魏王不

xiāng xìn　tā shuō　　nǐ de shè shù nán dào kě yǐ dá dào zhè yàng gāo chāo de
相信，他说："你的射术难道可以达到这样高超的

shuǐ píng ma　　gēng léi hěn zì xìn de shuō　　kě yǐ
水平吗？"更嬴很自信地说："可以。"

guò le yí huìr　　yì zhī yàn fēi guò lái　gēng léi ná qǐ gōng lā le
过了一会儿，一只雁飞过来，更嬴拿起弓拉了

31

一下空弦，那只雁就一下子栽落到地上。魏王惊叹说："你射箭的本领居然可以达到这样一种地步！"更赢说："这是一只受伤的孤雁啊！"魏王说："先生是怎么知道的呢？"更赢回答说："它飞得很缓慢，叫声很悲惨。飞得很慢，是因为它身上有旧伤疼痛；叫声很悲惨，是因为长久地离开了雁群，它感到孤独。由于它的伤口没有痊愈，而害怕的心情又没有去掉，所以一听见弓弦响，就急忙往高处飞，这就引起伤口破裂，它就从高空中跌落下来了。"

During the Warring States period, in the State of Wei there was a famous archer named Geng Lei. One day, standing on a dais, the king and Geng Lei looked up and saw a bird flying in the sky. Geng Lei said to the king, "My Lord, I can shoot down the bird by just drawing the bow without arrows." The king didn't believe him and asked, "Is your shooting skill so good?" Geng Lei replied confidently, "Yes, I am."

After a while, a goose flew by. Geng Lei pulled the empty string, and the goose fell to the ground all of a sudden. The king exclaimed, "Your archery is really so excellent!" Geng Lei said, "This is a wounded wild goose!" The king asked, "How did you know?" Geng Lei said, "It flew very slowly and cried sadly. It flew slowly because it had a wound in its body. It cried sadly because it felt lonely after being left behind the goose group. With the wound not healed and fear in its mind, it tried to fly up high after hearing the twang of the bowstring, and this caused the split of its wound. That's why it would fall from the sky."

故事寓意 | The moral of the story

"惊弓之鸟"用来形容受过惊吓或吃过亏的人碰到一点类似的事情就非常慌张害怕。这个故事告诉我们：要摒弃紧张、恐惧心理，勇敢面对一切，做一个乐观坚强的人。

"A bird startled by the twang of a bowstring" is used to express that people who have experienced frightening things or misfortunes would get panicked when confronted with such things. This story encourages us to overcome tension and fear, and to face all the challenges bravely.

鲲鹏与蓬雀

The Kunpeng and the Sparrows

chuán shuō zài zuì yáo yuǎn de běi fāng　qì hòu fēi cháng hán lěng　lián
传 说 在 最 遥 远 的 北 方，气 候 非 常 寒 冷，连

huā cǎo shù mù dōu bù shēng zhǎng　rén men bǎ nà ge dì fang jiào zuò　qióng
花 草 树 木 都 不 生 长，人 们 把 那 个 地 方 叫 作 "穷

fā　　zài nà lǐ yǒu yí piàn liáo kuò shuǐ yù xíng chéng de hú pō　lǐ miàn
发"。在 那 里 有 一 片 辽 阔 水 域 形 成 的 湖 泊，里 面

yǒu yì tiáo jù dà de yú　zhè tiáo yú de shēn tǐ yǒu jǐ qiān lǐ de kuān
有 一 条 巨 大 的 鱼。这 条 鱼 的 身 体 有 几 千 里 的 宽

dù　ér shēn tǐ de cháng dù ne　shéi yě shuō bù qīng chǔ　zhè tiáo dà yú
度，而 身 体 的 长 度 呢，谁 也 说 不 清 楚，这 条 大 鱼

de míng zi jiù jiào zuò kūn
的 名 字 就 叫 作 鲲。

有一天，这条大鱼变作了一只巨型的鸟。

它的脊背有泰山那样高大，双翅铺展开来，就像是挂在天空的白云，遮住了大半个天空，这只鸟名叫鹏。这只大鹏鸟打算从北海飞到南海，它扇动起两个巨大的翅膀，盘旋而上卷起一股狂风，它一直飞到九万里的高空，那是一个连云气都达不到的地方。大鹏的脊背几乎是紧靠着天的穹顶了，然后它朝南海的方向飞去。

有一群形体很小的蓬雀，它们长年在灌木丛中玩乐。当它们听说大鹏鸟飞到九万里高空后，非常惊讶与困惑，它们讥笑道："简直是疯了，它干吗要飞那么高呢？它到底想干什么呢？"其中一只蓬雀以不屑的口吻笑着说："我用力跳跃着向上一飞，也不过几丈

<pre>
gāo jiù luò xià lái   wǒ zài guàn mù cóng zhōng fēi lái fēi qù   zì yóu
高 就 落 下 来。 我 在 灌 木 丛 中 飞 来 飞 去, 自 由

kuài huo   zhè jiù shì shì jiè shang zuì hǎo de fēi xiáng le   nà zhī dà
快 活, 这 就 是 世 界 上 最 好 的 飞 翔 了。 那 只 大

péng niǎo zhè me qí guài   gān má yào fēi nà me gāo ne   fēi nà me gāo
鹏 鸟 这 么 奇 怪, 干 吗 要 飞 那 么 高 呢? 飞 那 么 高

yǒu shén me yì si ne
有 什 么 意 思 呢?"
</pre>

Legend has it that in the most distant north, the weather was very cold, and even the flowers and trees could not grow. So people called it "poor hair". In a large lake, there was a huge fish whose body was thousands of *li* in width and immeasurable in length. Its name was Kun.

One day, the fish turned into a huge bird whose back was as huge as Mount Taishan. When it spread its wings, it looked like a cloud that covered half of the sky. The bird's name was Peng. One day, the bird decided to fly from the North Sea to the South Sea. Flapping its huge wings and circling up with a strong upward gust, it flew up to 90,000 *li* in altitude, where even the clouds couldn't reach. The Peng's back was near the top of the sky, and then it flew toward the South Sea.

There was a group of little sparrows who played in the bushes all year round. When they heard that the Peng flew up to

90,000 *li*，they were shocked and confused. They sneered，"It's crazy. Why would it fly so high? What does it want to do?" One of the little birds said，"I jump up for several feet and then fall down. I just fly to and fro in the bush freely and happily. This is the best flying in the world. Why does Peng bother to fly that high? What's the point?"

故事寓意 | The moral of the story

小蓬雀不能理解鲲鹏的行为,反而讥笑鲲鹏,是因为小蓬雀的智慧和见识的肤浅。这个故事用来比喻浅薄无知的人不懂有高远理想和志向的人。有诗云:"会当凌绝顶,一览众山小。"只有登高望远的人,才知道世界有多么广大。

Little sparrows laughed at Kunpeng because they cannot understand its behavior，and this just shows the sparrows' shallowness and ignorance. The story satirizes shallow people who could not understand people with great expectations and ambitions. There is such a line in a Chinese poem，"I must ascend the mountain's crest; it dwarfs all peaks under my feet." Only people who climb high could know how vast the world is.

曲高和寡

Highbrow Songs Find Few Singers

zhàn guó shí qī   chǔ guó yǒu yí wèi zhù míng de wén xué jiā   míng jiào
战国时期，楚国有一位著名的文学家，名叫

sòng yù   pǐn xíng qīng gāo   xìng qíng dàn bó   tā céng jīng yǒu yí duàn shí jiān
宋玉，品行清高，性情淡泊。他曾经有一段时间

zuò wéi qǐng xiāng wáng de móu shì   shòu dào qǐng xiāng wáng de ēn chǒng
作为顷襄王的谋士，受到顷襄王的恩宠。

yí cì   qǐng xiāng wáng zhào jiàn sòng yù   shuō   zhè duàn shí jiān jīng
一次，顷襄王召见宋玉，说："这段时间经

cháng yǒu rén shuō nǐ de huài huà   nǐ shì yǒu yì xiē xíng wéi bù tuǒ dàng
常有人说你的坏话，你是有一些行为不妥当

ma   sòng yù huí dá shuō   shì de   yǒu zhè huí shì   qǐng dà wáng kuān
吗？"宋玉回答说："是的，有这回事。请大王宽

恕我，听我讲个故事：在先王的时代，有位歌唱

家来到楚国的郢都。他开始唱的是非常通俗的

歌曲，有几千人跟着他唱；接着，他唱起了比较

通俗的民谣，这时能跟着唱的有几百人；后来他

唱高雅歌曲，城里跟他唱的只有几十个人了；最

后，他唱出格调高雅的商音、羽音，又杂以流利

的徵音，创造出格调高雅、令人陶醉的音乐，能

够跟着哼唱的人更少，只有几个人了。""由此可

见，唱的曲子格调越是高雅，能跟着唱的也就

越少。圣人有奇伟的思想和行为，他的才能超

出普通人。一般人又怎能理解我的所作所

为呢？"

顷襄王听了，说："是呀！我明白了！"

During the Warring States period, in the State of Chu there was a famous scholar named Song Yu who held himself aloof and placid. For a while he was favored and chosen by King Qingxiang as his counsellor.

Once King Qingxiang summoned Song Yu and told him, "Recently, a lot of people say something bad about you. Did you do something improper?" Song Yu replied, "Yes, I did. Please pardon me, and let me tell you a story. In the time of the former Emperor, a singer came to the capital of Chu, Ying. He started to sing the most popular songs, and thousands of people joined him in singing. Then he sang the popular ballad, and about hundreds of people could follow him. Later he sang elegant songs, and only dozens of people could sing together. Finally he sang the most elegant tone, creating an intoxicating musical world, but only several could sing along. This shows that the more elegant the song, the fewer people could sing along. The saints usually have great minds and behaviors which are different from ordinary people. How could normal people understand what I do?"

After hearing this, the king exclaimed, "Ah, yes! Now I see."

故事寓意 | The moral of the story

"曲高和寡"用来形容圣人的言行超于常人，普通人难以理解、随同附和。这个故事告诉我们：一方面要追求至真至善的境界；另一方面，也要密切联系现实生活，不要自命清高，孤芳自赏。

"Highbrow songs find few singers" is used to describe that words and deeds of saints are hard to be understood by common people. This story tells us that on the one hand we should try to pursue the highest level of truth and ability, and on the other hand we should be connected to the realistic life and not indulge in self-admiration.

龙王与青蛙

Dragon King and the Frog

chuán shuō lóng wáng zhù zài hǎi dǐ shēn chù　tā néng hū fēng huàn yǔ
传说龙王住在海底深处,它能呼风唤雨,

xiǎng yǒu hěn gāo de dì wèi
享有很高的地位。

　　yì tiān　lóng wáng wài chū xún yóu　zài hǎi àn biān yù dào le yì zhī
一天,龙王外出巡游,在海岸边遇到了一只

qīng wā　qīng wā hěn hào qí lóng wáng zhù zài shén me yàng de dì fang　yú
青蛙。青蛙很好奇龙王住在什么样的地方,于

shì wèn dào　lóng wáng　nín jū zhù de dì fang shì zěn yàng de ya　lóng
是问道:"龙王,您居住的地方是怎样的呀?"龙

wáng huí dá　wǒ zhù zài hǎi dǐ de huáng gōng　shì yòng zhēn zhū　bèi ké
王回答:"我住在海底的皇宫,是用珍珠、贝壳

jiàn zào qǐ lái de　lǐ miàn huá lì gāo guì、jīn bì huī huáng　lóng wáng fǎn
建造起来的,里面华丽高贵、金碧辉煌。"龙王反

wèn qīng wā　nà me nǐ jū zhù de dì fang yòu shì shén me yàng zi ne
问青蛙:"那么你居住的地方又是什么样子呢?"

青蛙回答说："我住在山间的小溪边。风景美极了，那里有绿绿的草地、潺潺的流水和美丽的山石!"说着说着，青蛙开心地笑了起来。

青蛙再问龙王："龙王，您高兴和发怒的时候是怎样的呢?"龙王说："我高兴的时候，就在大地需要雨水的时候降下雨水，使大地滋润，五谷丰登;我发怒的时候，就刮狂风下暴雨，雷电交加，洪水淹没大地。"说完，龙王又问青蛙说："你在高兴和发怒的时候是怎样的?"青蛙回答说："我跟您完全不一样。我高兴了，就在云淡风清的时候唱歌跳舞，'呱呱'地叫上一阵;我要是发怒了，就先睁大眼睛凸出眼珠子，接着肚皮被气涨得鼓鼓的，最后气消了，肚子也干瘪下去了，什么事都过去了。"

Legend has it that Dragon King lived in the deep bottom of the ocean, and he enjoyed high status because he could summon wind and rain.

One day, Dragon King came out and met a frog along the coast. The frog was curious about the place where the Dragon King lived, so he asked the Dragon King, "Dragon King, what does your living place look like?" Dragon King replied, "I live in the palace at the bottom of the sea which is built with pearls and shells. It is noble and magnificent." And then he asked the frog, "How about your place?" The frog replied, "I live on the edge of a mountain stream with beautiful scenery. There are green grass, gurgling streams and beautiful rocks." Thinking about that, the frog couldn't help smiling happily.

The frog asked again, "Dragon King, how is it when you feel happy or angry?" Dragon King said, "When I am happy, it will rain in places where need it, and the rain will nourish the earth and guarantee the harvest. When I am angry, there will be violent storms, thunders and lightning, and the cataclysm will flood the entire world." Then Dragon King asked the frog, "How is it when you feel happy or angry?" The frog replied, "It's totally different from your situation. When I'm happy, I would sing and dance in the pure breeze and croak for a while. If I am angry, I would open my eyes wide and protrude eyeballs, then my belly will bulge. But finally I would feel peaceful, my belly would turn flat and everything would just be gone."

故事寓意 | **The moral of the story**

　　龙王和青蛙各有各的世界,各有各的活法,没有必要一味地羡慕别人。这个故事告诉我们:世间万事万物差别很大,重要的是要有自知之明,去做自己喜欢做的事,做自己能做的事。

　　Dragon King and the frog have their own worlds and different ways of living. There is no need to feel jealous about others blindly. This story tells us that everything in the world is different, and it is important to know yourself, to do what you like and what you can.

人穷志不短

Poor but with Lofty Ideals

chūn qiū shí qī   wú guó de gōng zǐ jì zhá yí gè rén chū mén yóu lì
春秋时期，吴国的公子季札一个人出门游历。

yì tiān   tā zhèng zǒu zài lù shang   hū rán kàn jiàn yí chuàn tóng qián   jì zhá
一天，他正走在路上，忽然看见一串铜钱，季札

xiǎng bǎ qián jiǎn qǐ lái   dàn yòu jué de wān yāo qù jiǎn qián yǒu shī shēn fèn
想把钱捡起来，但又觉得弯腰去捡钱有失身份。

pèng qiǎo   zhè shí yǒu gè tiāo zhe yí dàn zi chái huo de rén zǒu guò lái   jì
碰巧，这时有个挑着一担子柴火的人走过来。季

zhá xīn xiǎng   jiào zhè rén bǎ qián jiǎn qǐ lái   tā yí dìng huì shí fēn gǎn jī
札心想，叫这人把钱捡起来，他一定会十分感激，

tā tiāo de nà liǎng kǔn chái hái wèi jiàn dé zhí zhè me duō qián ne
他挑的那两捆柴还未见得值这么多钱呢。

děng nà tiāo chái de rén zǒu dào gēn qián shí   jì zhá fā xiàn xiàn zài suī
等那挑柴的人走到跟前时，季札发现现在虽

rán yǐ jīng shì wǔ yuè fèn le   dàn shì nà tiāo chái de rén jìng rán hái chuān zhe
然已经是五月份了，但是那挑柴的人竟然还穿着

46

冬天的皮袄。季札认为这个人一定很贫穷，让他

把钱捡去正合适。于是，季札大声地朝那个挑

柴人喊道："喂，你快来把地上的钱拾起来。"挑

柴人看着季札一副傲慢的样子，非常生气，他

说："你是谁？凭什么居高临下看不起人？我既然

能在炎热的夏天穿着皮袄去打柴，难道我会是个

贪图钱财的人吗？"

季札听了，连忙向他道歉，打柴人不再理睬

季札，对地上的钱连看都没看一眼就走了。季札

看着打柴人的背影，十分惭愧。

During the Spring and Autumn period, Zha, the fourth son of the King of the State of Wu went out to travel. One day, when walking on the road, suddenly he saw a string of copper coins on the ground. He wanted to pick it up but felt shameful to bend over to do it. Right then a man carried a load of firewood came near, and Zha thought that the man would be very grateful if he told him to pick the coins up because the coins overpriced all his firewood.

Zha waited until the man came near and he found that the man was wearing a winter coat although it was already May. So Zha thought this person must be very poor and it was appropriate to let him fetch the money. Therefore he shouted, "Hey, you come and pick up the money on the ground." The man carrying the wood was very angry at Zha's arrogance, and he said, "Who are you? How could you be so arrogant and look down upon others? I would go to cut wood in the hot summer in a fur coat. Would I be a mercenary man?"

Zha hurried to apologize, but the man didn't pay any attention and left without looking at the money on the ground. Watching the woodcutter's back, Zha was extremely ashamed of himself.

故事寓意 | The moral of the story

季札的浅薄与无礼，以至于遭到那个挑柴人的反唇相讥。这个故事告诉我们：不要以貌取人，首先要尊重别人，才能赢得别人的尊重。

Zha's *superficiality and rudeness was answered back sarcastically by the wood carrier. This story tells us that we should not judge people by their appearance. We must respect others in the first place so as to win the respect of others.*

螳螂挡车

A Mantis Trying to Obstruct the Wheel of a Chariot

yǒu yí cì   qí zhuāng gōng dài zhe jǐ shí míng shì wèi jìn shān dǎ
有一次，齐 庄 公 带着 几 十 名 侍 卫 进 山 打

liè   yí lù shang   qí zhuāng gōng xìng zhì bó bó   yǔ shì wèi men tán xiào
猎。一 路 上，齐 庄 公 兴 致 勃 勃，与 侍 卫 们 谈 笑

fēng shēng   zǒu zhe zǒu zhe   hū rán fā xiàn dào lù zhōng jiān yǒu yì zhī lǜ
风 生。走 着 走 着，忽 然 发 现 道 路 中 间 有 一 只 绿

sè de xiǎo kūn chóng   tā nù qì chōng chōng de jǔ qǐ liǎng zhī qián zú   sì
色 的 小 昆 虫，它 怒 气 冲 冲 地 举 起 两 只 前 足，似

hū yào gēn chē lún bó dòu
乎 要 跟 车 轮 搏 斗。

xiǎo xiǎo yì zhī chóng zi   jìng rán gǎn yǔ páng dà de chē lún jiào liàng
小 小 一 只 虫 子，竟 然 敢 与 庞 大 的 车 轮 较 量，

nà qíng jǐng shí fēn gǎn rén   zhè yǒu qù de chǎng miàn yǐn qǐ le qí zhuāng
那 情 景 十 分 感 人。这 有 趣 的 场 面 引 起 了 齐 庄

gōng de xìng qù   tā wèn shì wèi zhè shì shén me   shì wèi huí dá shuō   zhè
公 的 兴 趣，他 问 侍 卫 这 是 什 么，侍 卫 回 答 说："这

shì yì zhī táng láng   tā yào hé wǒ men de chē zi bó dòu   tā bù xiǎng ràng
是 一 只 螳 螂。它 要 和 我 们 的 车 子 搏 斗，它 不 想 让

我们过去呢。"齐庄公又问:"噫!真有趣。为什么会这样呢?"侍卫回答说:"大王,这种小虫,只知道往前冲,不知道向后退,它不衡量自己有多大力量,却往往轻视对手。"

听了这番话后,庄公再仔细地把螳螂打量一番,然后感慨地说道:"小小虫儿,志气不小。它要是人的话,一定将成为无敌于天下的勇士。"说完,他吩咐车夫勒住马头,将马车绕道行驶,不要压死它。

后来,齐国的将士们听说了这件事,都非常感动。从此,他们打起仗来更加奋不顾身,都愿以死来效忠齐庄公。

According to the legend, King Zhuang of the State of Qi once went hunting with dozens of guards. Along the way, the king laughed and talked with his guards. While then there was a small green insect standing in the middle of the road, raising its two front feet high furiously, as if it was going to fight against the wheels of the chariot.

A tiny insect dared to fight against huge wheels. What a touching picture! The interesting scene aroused the king's interest, so he asked the guard what it was. The guard answered, "It is a mantis. It seems that it's fighting with our wheels because it doesn't want us to pass." The king continued to ask, "Wow, that's interesting. But why?" The guard replied, "My Lord, the little insect just knows how to move forward but not how to retreat. It has no idea about its own power and is scornful of its opponents."

After hearing this, King Zhuang observed the mantis carefully and then said, "A small insect with respectable ambition. If it were a man, it would be an invincible warrior." Then he ordered the driver to rein in the horse and change their way, so as not to roll over it.

Later, all the soldiers of the State of Qi were greatly touched after they knew the story. From then on, they would like to fight even more bravely for the king.

生难字/词注解 | Note

谈笑风生：形容谈话时有说有笑，兴致很高，并且很风趣。

Tan xiao feng sheng (laughed and talked)： Talk cheerfully and humorously.

故事寓意 | The moral of the story

"螳螂挡车"后人常作"螳臂挡车"，用来比喻不估计自己的力量，去做办不到的事情。这个故事告诉我们：要认清形势，去做自己力所能及的事情。

"A mantis trying to obstruct the wheel of a chariot" refers to people who do not know about their own strength and try to do impossible things. The story tells us that we should have a clear understanding of the situation and do things according to our capabilities.

铁棒磨成针

Grinding an Iron Rod into a Sewing Needle

táng dài yǒu yí gè zhù míng shī rén míng jiào lǐ bái　　tā xiǎo shí hou

唐代有一个著名诗人名叫李白。他小时候

bù zhuān xīn dú shū　cháng cháng táo xué qù wán　　yì tiān　lǐ bái yòu méi

不专心读书，常 常 逃学去玩。一天，李白又没

yǒu qù shàng xué　tā zài jiē shang wán shuǎ　zǒu zhe zǒu zhe　kàn jiàn yí wèi

有去上学。他在街上玩耍，走着走着，看见一位

lǎo pó po zài mó dāo shí shang mó zhe yì gēn cū dà de tiě bàng　　lǐ bái

老婆婆在磨刀石上磨着一根粗大的铁棒。李白

hěn hào qí　jiù còu guò qù wèn　lǎo pó po　nín zài zuò shén me　　mó

很好奇，就凑过去问："老婆婆，您在做什么？""磨

zhēn　lǎo pó po tóu yě méi tái　jiǎn dān de huí dá le lǐ bái　yī rán rèn

针。"老婆婆头也没抬，简单地回答了李白，依然认

zhēn de mó zhe shǒu lǐ de tiě bàng　　mó zhēn　lǐ bái jué de hěn bù kě

真地磨着手里的铁棒。"磨针？"李白觉得很不可

sī yì　rěn bú zhù yòu wèn　lǎo pó po　zhēn shì fēi cháng xì xiǎo de　ér

思议，忍不住又问："老婆婆，针是非常细小的，而

nín mó de shì yì gēn cū dà de tiě bàng ya　zhè shí hou　lǎo pó po cái

您磨的是一根粗大的铁棒呀！"这时候，老婆婆才

抬起头来，慈祥地望着小李白，说："是的，铁棒又粗又大，要把它磨成针是很困难的。可是我每天不停地磨呀磨，总有一天，我会把它磨成针的。孩子，只要功夫下得深，铁棒也能磨成针呀！"

此时，李白年纪虽小，却是个悟性很高的孩子，他听了老婆婆的话之后，非常惭愧。他赶紧回去读书，从此再也没有逃过学。他通过坚持不渝地努力，最后终于成了名扬天下的"诗仙"。

In the Tang Dynasty, there was a famous poet named Li Bai. When he was a little boy, he disliked studying and often played truant. One day, he didn't go to school but played on the street. He saw an old granny grinding an iron rod on a big stone when he was walking. Out of curiosity, Li Bai came up and asked, "What are you doing, granny?" "I'm grinding an iron rod," said the old women without stopping grinding. "Grinding?" Li Bai felt unbelievable and couldn't help asking, "Granny, a needle is very thin，but you're grinding so big a rod." Then the granny raised her head and looked at Li Bai genially，saying，"Yes，the rod is huge and thick，and it's hard to grind it into a needle. But as long as I keep grinding，certainly someday I'll make it. Little boy，with patience and time，a rod can be turned into a needle."

Although Li Bai was still a little boy，he was very smart. He felt ashamed of himself and quickly returned to school to study and never skipped classes again. Through his constant efforts，he finally became one of the most outstanding poets well known in the world.

故事寓意 | **The moral of the story**

这个故事告诉我们：无论做什么事情,都要有恒心,通过坚持不懈地努力,终有一天会实现理想。

This story tells us that no matter what we do，we must be perseverant，and through persistent efforts one day we will make our dreams come true.

向日葵和石头

The Sunflower and the Stone

zhǒng zi chéng shú le　　luò dào ní tǔ lǐ miàn　rán hòu fā yá　shēng
种子成熟了，落到泥土里面，然后发芽、生

zhǎng　　 zhè yuán běn shì yí jiàn hěn zì rán　hé lǐ de shì qing　　kě shì
长。这原本是一件很自然、合理的事情。可是，

yǒu yí lì zhǒng zi què yīn cǐ dé zuì le yí kuài shí tou　　jù shuō nà shì
有一粒种子却因此得罪了一块石头。据说那是

yí kuài nián suì hěn dà de shí tou　tā xǐ ài ān jìng　xǐ huān sī kǎo wèn
一块年岁很大的石头，它喜爱安静，喜欢思考问

tí　 yǒu yì tiān　dāng tā zhèng zài sī kǎo wèn tí de shí hou　　hū rán yǒu
题。有一天，当它正在思考问题的时候，忽然有

yí lì zhǒng zi　wèi jīng tā de xǔ kě　　luò zài le tā de páng biān　tā wèi
一粒种子，未经它的许可，落在了它的旁边，它为

cǐ shí fēn shēng qì
此十分生气。

56

这块石头下定决心要把种子赶走。它每天诅咒种子被风刮走、被雨水冲走、被烈日晒死。可不管它怎样做，种子一直都好好地待在那儿。过了几天，种子长出了新嫩的芽儿。石头简直气坏了，它说："等着瞧吧！你生出来没几天，个儿小，又不结实，你活不了多久的！"种子没有理会石头，而是自由自在地呼吸、生长。它越长越壮实，越长越高。石头更加气愤了，它恨不得每天刮风下雨，把种子摧毁。

可是，顽强的种子忍受住了风吹雨打。春天来了，太阳变得温暖，雨水也十分充足，小嫩芽贪婪地吮吸着养分，逐渐长成了一株美丽的向日葵。石头看着那株向日葵，很不服气。它想：也许小向日葵还没长大就死了呢？也许，它再长高一点，就支持不住自己身体的重量，会突然倒下了呢？然而，小向日葵的根不断地扎往深处，它的茎变得更加结实、粗壮，叶子也长得更加茂盛。

终于有一天，小向日葵变成了大向日葵，开出了一朵大大的金黄色花盘。花盘一年四季始终向着太阳，不知疲倦地随着太阳转呀转呀。后来大向日葵结了许多种子，新的种子成熟了，又落到土壤里去，长出新的向日葵来。就这样循环往复，向日葵长满了整个山头。至于那块伤心的石头呢，它在寒来暑往，日复一日的风雨侵袭中慢慢地裂开了，最后散落成了泥土，变成了植物的养料。

It's natural and reasonable that ripe seeds would fall into the earth, and then germinate and grow. But a seed offended a stone this way. It is said that it was a very old stone. It enjoyed sitting quietly and pondering over questions. One day, when the stone was contemplating, a seed fell by its side without its permission, and this made the stone angry.

The stone was determined to drive the seed away. Every day the stone cursed that the seed would be blown away by the wind, washed away by the rain, and burnt by the sun. But whatever the stone did, the seed stayed there well. A few days later, the seed grew buds, the stone was angry and said, "Just wait and see. You were just born for a few days. You are small and frail, and soon you will die." The seed ignored the stone's words, breathing and growing freely. It grew stronger and stronger, taller and taller. The stone was even angrier and hoped that it would be rainy and windy every day and then the seed would be destroyed.

However, the seed was so strong that it put up with the wind and rain. When spring came, the sun became warm and there was plenty of rainwater. The small bud sucked the nutrients greedily, and gradually grew into a beautiful sunflower. The stone looked at the sunflower, feeling ill-affected. It thought that maybe the little sunflower would die before it completely grew up. Maybe, when it became taller, it could not support its own weight and collapse suddenly. However, the little sunflower made its root deepen into the earth, and its stem became more robust and its leaves also grew lushly.

Eventually, the little sunflower became a big sunflower and it bloomed. The flower disk faced the sun all year round, revolving with the sun without feeling tired. Afterwards，the big sunflower yielded many seeds，and when the seeds became ripe，again they fell into the earth and became new sunflowers. It kept going like this，and soon the hill was covered with sunflowers. The upset stone cracked in the wind and rain after several winters and summers，and finally collapsed into soil and turned into nutrients of the plant.

故事寓意 | The moral of the story

向日葵以顽强的意志生长，而石头却在妒忌与烦恼中生活。这个故事告诉我们：要以宽容平和的心态面对一切，顺应天地万物生存的自然法则，不悲不喜，成为最好的自己。

The sunflower keeps growing with a strong will，while the stone lives in jealousy and worry. This story tells us that we should face everything with peace and tolerance and follow the natural laws of the world. Do not get pleased or saddened by external things，and we shall bring the best out of ourselves.

眼盲心明

The Eyes Are Blind, but the Mind Is Clear

yǒu yí gè shào nián, tā shuāng yǎn shī míng le, dàn shì tā fēi cháng
有一个少年，他双眼失明了，但是，他非常

shàn cháng tán qín jī gǔ。 tā de lín jū shì yí gè dú shū rén。 yì tiān，
擅长弹琴击鼓。他的邻居是一个读书人。一天，

nà ge dú shū rén hé shào nián liáo tiān， tā duì shào nián shuō： nǐ yǎn jing shī
那个读书人和少年聊天，他对少年说："你眼睛失

míng yǐ jīng yǒu shí jǐ nián le， nǐ zhěng tiān gǎn shòu dào de dōu shì hēi àn，
明已经有十几年了，你整天感受到的都是黑暗，

bù zhī dào huā cǎo shù mù、 rì yuè shān chuān hé rén jiān shì xiàng， bù zhī dào
不知道花草树木、日月山川和人间世象，不知道

róng mào de měi chǒu hé fēng jǐng de xiù lì， qǐ bú shì tài kě bēi le ma？
容貌的美丑和风景的秀丽，岂不是太可悲了吗？"

少年回答说："你只知道盲人是盲的，而不知道不盲的人有时也大都是盲的。我虽然眼睛看不见，但身体和思想却是自由的。听声音我便知道是谁，听谈话能辨别是非。我热爱生活，全身心地投入自己喜欢的工作中，不浪费精力去应付那些无聊的事情。可是，你看当今社会上有些人虽然有眼睛，看得见世界，但他们的眼睛和心灵却被欲望蒙蔽了。他们颠倒是非，还有的人胡作非为，最后害人害己。这些人难道没有眼睛吗？那些睁着眼睛的人实际上也是盲人呀！他们比我这个生理上的盲人更可悲呀！"

那个读书人听了，竟无言以对。

Once there was a boy who was blind but good at playing the ancient Chinese zithers and the drums. His neighbor was a scholar. One day, when they were chatting, the scholar chatted to the boy, "You have been blind for more than ten years. All you can feel is the darkness, and you know nothing about the flowers and trees, mountains and rivers, and all the sceneries in the world. Isn't it a pity for not knowing the beautiful faces and landscapes?"

The boy replied, "You just know that the blind people can't see, but you don't know that for most of the time people who aren't blind are also blind. Though I can't see, my body and mind are free. I can recognize people from their voices, make judgment from their conversations. I love life and I devote whole-heartedly to the job I like instead of wasting energy in coping with boring things. But, for some people who can see with their eyes, their eyes and hearts are blinded by desires. They confound right and wrong, behave outrageously, and eventually hurt others and themselves. Don't they have eyes? But they are also blind indeed. It is them who are more pathetic than people who are physically blind."

Hearing this, the scholar was speechless.

故事寓意 | The moral of the story

这个故事告诉我们：眼睛失明是身不由己的事情，但是，只要心里明辨是非，知晓礼义廉耻，就会比那些双眼明亮但不明事理的人更为值得尊敬与爱护。

This story tells us that losing sight is out of our control, but as long as we can judge right from wrong and be aware of the principles of honesty and integrity, we are more respectable than people who can see with eyes but not with hearts.

一毛不拔难为人

Not to Give Away Even a Hair

yǒu yì zhī hóu zi zhù zài shān lín lǐ　tā fēi cháng xiàn mù rén lèi
有一只猴子住在山林里，它非常美慕人类。

tā jué de　rén lèi shí zài tài kuài lè le　　guǒ shí chéng shú de shí hou　tā
它觉得，人类实在太快乐了。果实成熟的时候，他

men kě yǐ zhāi xià lái yì luó kuāng yì luó kuāng de tiāo dào jiā lǐ qù　bù xiàng
们可以摘下来一箩筐一箩筐地挑到家里去，不像

hóu zi　yì nián dào tóu dōu zài sì chù bēn bō　xún zhǎo shí wù　dào le hán lěng
猴子，一年到头都在四处奔波，寻找食物；到了寒冷

de dōng tiān　rén men kě yǐ zhù zài shū shì wēn nuǎn de fáng wū lǐ kǎo huǒ　chī
的冬天，人们可以住在舒适温暖的房屋里烤火，吃

zhe měi wèi de shí wù　　bù jǐn rú cǐ　měi yí hù rén jiā dōu chǔ bèi le dà
着美味的食物。不仅如此，每一户人家都储备了大

liàng guò dōng de liáng shi　bù xiàng hóu zi　yí dào dōng tiān　jiù zhǐ néng zhù zài
量过冬的粮食，不像猴子，一到冬天，就只能住在

lěng bīng bīng de shí dòng lǐ　yòu lěng yòu è　zhè zhī hóu zi xiǎng dào zhè xiē
冷冰冰的石洞里，又冷又饿。这只猴子想到这些

就很伤心，它发誓来世一定不做猴子。

后来，这只猴子真的死了，它到阴间拜见阎王。阎王问猴子说："来世你还想做猴吗？"猴子连忙说："我不想做猴了，做猴子太辛苦了，请大王把我变成人吧！"阎王说："好，我就遂了你的心愿。不过想变成人有个条件，那就是你必须将身上的毛发全部拔掉。"

说完，阎王命令一个小鬼给猴子拔毛。可是刚拔了一根毛，猴子就痛得大叫起来："哎哟，哎哟，受不了，受不了！我不拔了，不拔了！"小鬼让它忍耐一下，安慰它说很快就好了。猴子哭丧着脸说："太痛了，我实在无法忍受这种痛苦！"

这时，阎王笑着对猴子说："看你连一根毛都舍不得拔，怎么能成为人呢？"意思是这只猴子活着的时候只看到了人的快乐，却没有看到人类付出

de jiān xīn hé hàn shuǐ　　yào xiǎng yǒu suǒ shōu huò　　bì rán yǒu suǒ fù chū
的 艰 辛 和 汗 水 。 要 想 有 所 收 获 ， 必 然 有 所 付 出 。

xiàng hóu zi zhè yàng yì gēn máo fà dōu bù shě dé bá　　yì diǎnr　　kǔ dōu
像 猴 子 这 样 一 根 毛 发 都 不 舍 得 拔 ， 一 点 儿 苦 都

shòu bù liǎo　　zěn me néng chéng wéi rén ne
受 不 了 ， 怎 么 能 成 为 人 呢 ？

A monkey lived in the mountains, and it was very jealous of mankind because it thought that human beings lived in a joyful way. When fruits were ripe, they could bring lots of them to home in baskets. While monkeys had to search for food all year around, sometimes they could be full and sometimes not. In the cold winter, people could stay in their own warm houses with the whole family and eat delicious food, and every family had enough food preserved for the whole winter. While monkeys, when winter came, they could only huddle in the cave, suffering coldness and hunger. The monkey felt sad and swore that in the afterlife it would no longer be a monkey.

Later, the monkey really died. It went to the nether world to see the King of Hell. The King of Hell asked the monkey, "In the future world, do you still want to be a monkey?" The monkey quickly said, "I don't want to be a monkey. It's pathetic to be monkey. Please let me become a real man!" The King of Hell said, "OK, I'll change you to a person as you wish with one requirement. You need to give away all your body hair."

Then, King of Hell ordered one goblin to pluck out the monkey's hair. But just after being pulled out one single hair, the monkey cried, "Oh, I cannot stand, cannot stand." The goblin required the monkey to put up with it for a moment and comforted it that soon the plucking would be over, but the monkey said miserably, "It's too painful for me to stand it!"

The King of Hell smiled and said to the monkey, "If you are not willing to have one single hair plucked, how can you become a human being?" It means that when the monkey was alive, it just noticed the happiness of mankind but didn't know that their happiness was obtained through hard work. The monkey couldn't put up with the pain of getting plucked. Then how can it become a human being?

故事寓意 | The moral of the story

"一毛不拔"用来形容一个人十分小气吝啬和自私,不愿与他人分享。这个故事告诉我们:做人要勤劳、宽容和善良。用辛勤劳动来换取幸福生活;用宽容大度赢得他人的尊重;用善良之心来收获永恒的情谊。

"Not to give away even a hair" is used to describe stingy and selfish people who would not like to share with others. This story tells us that we should be industrious, tolerant and kind. We should pursue a happy life through hard work, win respect by tolerance and harvest friendship with a kind heart.

中

国

经

典

寓

言

故

事

第二辑

Part 2

扁鹊说病

Bianque's Ideas about Treating Illness

chūn qiū shí qī　yǒu yí wèi zhù míng de　yī shī　rén men dōu jiào tā
春 秋 时 期 , 有 一 位 著 名 的 医 师 , 人 们 都 叫 他

biǎn què　　biǎn què yī shù gāo míng　jīng cháng chū rù gōng tíng wèi jūn wáng zhì
扁 鹊 。 扁 鹊 医 术 高 明 , 经 常 出 入 宫 廷 为 君 王 治

bìng　　yǒu yì tiān　biǎn què qù cháo jiàn cài huán gōng　jīng guò xì xīn guān
病 。 有 一 天 , 扁 鹊 去 朝 见 蔡 桓 公 , 经 过 细 心 观

chá　fā xiàn huán gōng huàn yǒu pí fū bìng　jiàn yì tā jí shí zhì liáo　huán
察 , 发 现 桓 公 患 有 皮 肤 病 , 建 议 他 及 时 治 疗 。 桓

gōng tīng shuō hòu　bìng bù xiāng xìn
公 听 说 后 , 并 不 相 信 。

shí tiān yǐ hòu　biǎn què dì èr cì qù jiàn huán gōng　tā chá kàn le
十 天 以 后 , 扁 鹊 第 二 次 去 见 桓 公 , 他 察 看 了

huán gōng de liǎn sè zhī hòu shuō　nín de bìng dào jī ròu lǐ miàn qù le
桓 公 的 脸 色 之 后 说 :"您 的 病 到 肌 肉 里 面 去 了 。

如果不治疗，病情还会加重。"桓公还是不相信。又过了十天，扁鹊第三次去见桓公，他看了看桓公，说道："您的病已经发展到肠胃里面去了。如果不赶紧医治，病情将会恶化。"桓公非常生气。又隔了十天，扁鹊第四次去见桓公。两人刚一见面，扁鹊什么话也没有说，很快就走了。

桓公十分奇怪，派人去问原因，扁鹊说："一开始桓公皮肤患病，用汤药清洗、热敷容易治愈；稍后他的病到了肌肉里面，用针灸可以医治；后来桓公的病到了肠胃，服草药汤剂还有疗效。可是现在他的病到了骨髓，已经没有办法医治了。"

五天过后，桓公浑身疼痛，派人去寻找扁鹊，发现扁鹊已经逃走了。桓公这时非常后悔，后来他在病痛的折磨下死去了。

During the Spring and Autumn period, there was a famous doctor named Bianque. He was remarkable for his excellent medical skills, and thus he was summoned to the court to take care of the Duke. One day, Bianque went to see Duke Huan of the State of Cai. After careful observation, he found that Duke Huan was suffering from a skin disease and advised him to get treated instantly. Duke Huan did not believe him at all. Ten days later, Bianque paid a second visit to the Duke and said, "The disease is spreading into your skin. If it is not cured, I'm afraid it will get worse." The Duke still didn't believe him. Another ten days passed by before he paid a third visit, and he told the Duke, "Now the disease has reached your intestines and stomach. If it is not cured, I'm afraid it will worsen." Once again, he encountered Duke's displeasure. Another ten days fled away before Bianque came to see the Duke for the fourth time, and he ran away without saying anything.

The Duke felt extremely surprised and sent a guard to inquire him. Bianque explained, "When the disease is on the skin, it can be cured by hot compress of medicine. When it slips beneath the skins, it can be healed by acupuncture. When it comes to the intestines and stomach, it still can be treated with herbal medicine and hot drug soups. The disease has come to the Duke's spine, and now it is at the hands of God and there is nothing I can do."

Five days later, Duke felt painful all over his body and sent for Bianque who had already run away. Duke Huan felt so regretful then, and was tortured by illness tragically till death.

生难字/词注解 | Notes

恶化：情况向坏的方面变化，使更坏。

Worsen：Take a turn for the worse.

热敷：用热的物体如热水袋或热毛巾置于痛处来消除或减轻疼痛。

Hot compress：Hot pack，put hot staff such as hot towel or hot-water bag to ease the pain.

故事寓意 | The moral of the story

这个故事告诉我们：对于疾病不要忌讳，应该高度重视，及时医治。否则，等到病情非常严重，就没有药可以疗救了。

This story tells us that we should not avoid admitting our diseases which should get our full attention and be cured timely. Otherwise, when the diseases become more serious, nothing can be done to save our lives.

唇亡齿寒

If the Lips Are Gone, the Teeth Will Be Cold

chūn qiū shí qī   jìn xiàn gōng dǎ suàn chū bīng gōng dǎ guó guó   dàn shì
春秋时期，晋献公打算出兵攻打虢国，但是

bì xū jīng guò yú guó   tā dān xīn yú guó bù dā ying jiè lù ràng tā de jūn
必须经过虞国，他担心虞国不答应借路让他的军

duì guò qù   zhè shí   jìn guó dà chén xún xī duì xiàn gōng shuō   yú guó guó
队过去。这时，晋国大臣荀息对献公说："虞国国

jūn shì gè mù guāng duǎn qiǎn   tān tú xiǎo lì de rén   zhǐ yào wǒ men sòng
君是个目光短浅、贪图小利的人。只要我们送

tā jià zhí áng guì de měi yù hé bǎo mǎ   tā jiù huì dā ying jiè lù de   jìn
他价值昂贵的美玉和宝马，他就会答应借路的。"晋

xiàn gōng yǒu diǎn shě bù dé měi yù hé bǎo mǎ   xún xī kàn chū le jìn xiàn
献公有点舍不得美玉和宝马。荀息看出了晋献

公的心思，就说："虞、虢两个国家是关系密切的近邻，虢国被消灭了，虞国也不能独自存在，您的美玉、宝马不过是暂时存放在虞国公那里罢了。"

于是，晋献公采纳了荀息的计策。虞国国君见到美玉和宝马这两件珍贵的礼物，十分高兴。当他听荀息说要借虞国的道路时，就很爽快地答应了。但是，虞国大臣宫之奇听说后，赶快阻止道："这可不行呀，我们虞国和虢国相互依存，相互帮助。万一虢国灭亡了，我们虞国也就难保了。俗话说：'唇亡齿寒'，没有嘴唇，牙齿是会挨冻的呀。"可是，虞国国君贪图晋国的礼物，没有听从劝阻。果然，晋国凭借兵强马壮，很快就消灭了虢国，随后又消灭了虞国。

During the Spring and Autumn period, Duke Xian of the State of Jin wanted to send troops to destroy the State of Guo. But there was a third state, the State of Yu located between Jin and Guo, and the Jin's army had to cross the State of Yu before it reached the State of Guo. Then his minister Xun Xi suggested, "The Emperor of the State of Yu is short-sighted and covets small advantages. If we give him priceless precious stones and fine horses, he will definitely allow our army to pass through his state." Seeing that Duke Xian of the State of Jin was grudging, Xun Xi continued to say, "The State of Yu and the State of Guo are neighboring states. The State of Yu cannot exist independently if the State of Guo is destroyed. Your precious stones and fine horses are just left in the care of the Emperor of the State of Yu temporarily."

So Duke Xian of the State of Jin adopted Xun Xi's plan. When the Emperor of the State of Yu saw the precious gifts, he was so glad and readily promised to let Jin's army pass through his state. But hearing the news, Gong Zhiqi, one of the ministers of the State of Yu, hurried to stop the Emperor, saying, "That won't do. The State of Yu and the State of Guo are neighboring states. We two small states are interdependent and can help each other when problems crop up. If the State of Guo were destroyed, it would be difficult for State of Yu to continue to exist. As the common saying goes, if the lips are gone, the teeth will be cold. The teeth can hardly be kept if the lips are gone." But the Emperor of the State of Yu refused to accept his advice because he was greedy to take the presents from the State of Jin. As expected, the troops of the State of Jin destroyed the State of Guo, and then destroyed the State of Yu as well.

故事寓意 | The moral of the story

"唇亡齿寒"比喻双方关系密切,相互依存。这个故事告诉我们:做事要权衡轻重,不要贪图小利,以免带来灾祸。

The set phrase "if the lips are gone, the teeth will be cold" is used to describe the situation that two people or things share a common fate and depend on each other. The story tells us that we should balance loss and gain, and we shouldn't covet small profits lest disaster may follow.

东郭先生和狼

Mr. Dongguo and the Wolf

cóng qián　yǒu yí wèi dōng guō xiān sheng　　yì tiān tā qiān zhe máo lǘ chū
从前，有一位东郭先生。一天他牵着毛驴出

mén　máo lǘ de bèi shang hái tuó zhe yì kǒu dài shū　　hū rán　tā kàn jiàn yì
门，毛驴的背上还驮着一口袋书。忽然，他看见一

zhī shén sè huāng zhāng de láng pǎo guò lái　guì zài tā miàn qián shuō hòu miàn yǒu
只神色慌张的狼跑过来，跪在他面前说后面有

liè rén　qǐ qiú tā jiù mìng　dōng guō xiān sheng xīn ruǎn le　dā ying le láng
猎人，乞求他救命。东郭先生心软了，答应了狼

de qǐng qiú　tā bǎ kǒu dài lǐ de shū dōu dào le chū lái　ràng láng zuàn jìn qù
的请求，他把口袋里的书都倒了出来，让狼钻进去，

rán hòu bǎ dài kǒu jì jǐn le　dāng liè rén lái xún wèn yǒu méi yǒu kàn jiàn láng
然后把袋口系紧了。当猎人来询问有没有看见狼

de shí hou　dōng guō xiān sheng yáo yáo tóu　shuō　méi kàn jiàn　děng liè rén
的时候，东郭先生摇摇头，说："没看见。"等猎人

走远了，东郭先生解开袋口，把狼放了出来，狼却露出凶恶的本性，想要吃掉东郭先生。东郭先生十分生气，大声喊道："你这只恶狼，我刚才好心救了你的命，你现在却要吃我，你可真是忘恩负义呀"。

这时，走来了一位挂着藜杖的老人，东郭先生赶忙拉住老人，要老人评判谁有道理。狼为自己辩解："您别听他胡说八道，他刚才把我塞进口袋里，害得我在里面闷得喘不上气来，这样的人我不该把他吃掉吗？"老人想了想，说："你们都认为自己有理，我也不好判定谁是谁非。这样吧，你们把刚才的情形再做一遍让我看看。"

于是，狼又钻进了东郭先生的口袋里，东郭先生把袋口系得紧紧的。老人立刻举起拐杖狠狠地朝着狼打去。东郭先生这时才明白过来，老人救了他的命。

Once upon a time, there was a scholar named Dongguo. One day he went out with a donkey, and the donkey carried a bag of books on its back. Suddenly, a panicked wolf pursued by hunters ran over, kneeling down and begging for help. Softhearted, Mr. Dongguo promised to save it. He took the books out of his bag, put the wolf in and then fastened the bag. When the hunter came along and asked if he had seen a wolf, Mr. Dongguo shook his head and said, "No, I haven't seen a wolf." When the hunter was far gone, Mr. Dongguo untied the bag and let the wolf out, but the wolf exposed his true vicious nature and wanted to eat Mr. Dongguo. Mr. Dongguo was very angry, so he shouted, "What a vicious wolf. I just saved your life but now you're going to eat me. You are really ungrateful."

Then, came an old man leaning on a crutch. Mr. Dongguo pulled the old man and asked him to make a judgment. The wolf defended itself, "Don't listen to his bullshit. He jammed me into his bag and almost suffocated me. Shouldn't I eat such a bad person?" The old man thought over the situation for a few seconds and said, "Both of you think yourself were right. It's hard for me to judge. Well, show me what happened just now."

So the wolf got into the bag again and Mr. Dongguo tied the bag up as before. The old man immediately beat the wolf with his crutch. Only then did Mr. Dongguo come to realize that he was saved by the old man.

生难字/词注解 | Notes

黎杖：用藜的老茎做的手杖，质轻而坚实。

Crutch：Stick made of pigweed to support one's weight，light but solid.

辩解：指对受人指责的某种见解或行为加以申辩解释。

Defend：Argue in support of one's action or idea when they're criticized.

故事寓意 | The moral of the story

这个故事告诉我们：对恶人应该保持高度警惕，要明辨是非，立场坚定，以防止上当受骗。现在，"东郭先生"常常用来形容那些不辨是非而滥施同情心的人；"中山狼"是形容那些忘恩负义、恩将仇报的人。

This story tells us that we should be alert to wicked people and know how to distinguish right from wrong. We should have a firm stand and try not to be fooled. Now, "Mr. Dongguo" is often used to describe those who help others blindly without distinguishing right from wrong. "Zhongshan wolf" is used to describe those ungrateful people.

打草惊蛇

Beating the Grass and Startling the Snake

táng cháo de shí hou　yǒu yí gè míng jiào wáng lǔ de xiàn guān　tā
唐朝的时候，有一个名叫王鲁的县官，他

shí fēn tān lán　jīng cháng jiē shòu huì lù　móu qǔ sī lì　zài tā dān
十分贪婪，经常接受贿赂，谋取私利。在他担

rèn xiàn lìng qī jiān　zuò le xǔ duō shāng tiān hài lǐ　tān zāng wǎng fǎ de
任县令期间，做了许多伤天害理、贪赃枉法的

huài shì　sú huà shuō　shàng liáng bú zhèng xià liáng wāi　wáng lǔ shǔ
坏事。俗话说："上梁不正下梁歪。"王鲁属

xià de nà xiē dà xiǎo guān lì　jiàn wáng lǔ tān zāng wǎng fǎ　yě dōu yí
下的那些大小官吏，见王鲁贪赃枉法，也都一

gè gè míng mù zhāng dǎn de gàn huài shì　tā men shí cháng qiāo zhà lè
个个明目张胆地干坏事。他们时常敲诈勒

suǒ　tān wū shòu huì　dāng dì lǎo bǎi xìng yǒu yuān wú chù shēn　yǒu kǔ
索、贪污受贿。当地老百姓有冤无处伸，有苦

shuō bù chū　dà jiā xīn lǐ dōu xī wàng néng yǒu gè jī huì hǎo hǎo chéng zhì
说不出，大家心里都希望能有个机会好好惩治

83

他们。

一次，刚巧朝廷派遣钦差大臣来巡察地方官员情况。当地老百姓知道后，就一起联名写了检举信，控告县府里的书记官等人营私舞弊、贪污受贿。检举信首先呈送给县令王鲁审阅。

王鲁把信从头到尾看了一遍，非常恐惧，顿时脸色都变了。

原来，老百姓在检举信中列举的种种犯罪事实，和他自己平时的违法行为一模一样。其中，还有许多坏事都和自己有牵连。检举信虽是控告书记官几个人的，但是王鲁觉得就跟状告自己一样。他越想越觉得害怕，担心朝廷会知道实情。到那时，就真的要大祸临头了。

王鲁想着想着，惊恐的心怎么也安静不下来，他不由自主地用颤抖的手拿笔在案卷上写

xià le jǐ gè zì　　rǔ suī dǎ cǎo　wú yǐ jīng shé　　gāng xiě wán　tā jiù
下了几个字："汝虽打草,吾已惊蛇。"刚写完,他就

tān zuò zài yǐ zi shang　bǐ yě diào dào dì shang qù le
瘫坐在椅子上,笔也掉到地上去了。

During the Tang Dynasty，there was a county magistrate named Wang Lu who always took bribes. During his tenure as county magistrate，he did a lot of bad things such as taking bribes and breaking the law. As the saying goes，"If the upper beam is not straight，the lower ones will go aslant." A large number of his subordinates all followed him to take bribes and violate the law. There was nowhere for the local people to go for justice，so they all hoped there would be a chance to punish them.

Then，it happened that the court sent an imperial envoy to supervise local officials. When the local people knew this，they wrote a letter of accusation，accusing the secretary officer and other officers of engaging in malpractices and bribery violations. The letter of accusation was first sent to the county magistrate Wang Lu. He read the letter from the beginning to the end and felt very scared，and his face turned pale.

It turned out that the crimes cited in the prosecution letter were the same as his own illegal behaviors，and many of them had connection to himself. Although the letter of accusation just charged the secretary and other officers，Wang Lu felt like as if he had been sued. He became more and more anxious, being afraid that the court would find out the truth which would be a disaster to him.

He was so frightened and couldn't settle down. He couldn't help writing these words on the file with his shivering hand, "By beating the grass, you have startled me as if I am a snake under the grass." After writing these words, he collapsed into the chair and his brush fell to the ground.

故事寓意 | The moral of the story

这个故事告诉我们：为人处世要品行端正、光明磊落，只有行得端，立得正，才能心安理得，问心无愧。

This story tells us that we should be a man of integrity behaving in a proper and decent manner, and only in this way can we live with a clear conscience.

覆车之鉴

The Lesson of an Overturned Carriage

一位老师带着几名学生外出游玩，正好遇到天下大雨，他们走得很艰难。在路上他们看到一辆车子，正停在高高的山路上歇息。老师对学生们说："你们看，那辆车子没有多久肯定会翻掉的。"学生听了，十分疑惑，就问道："为什么呢？"老师说："你们看就是了。"说着，他们继续行路。

没过多久，忽然有一片喧闹声从山路那边传过来。他们惊奇地回头看时，那辆车子果然已经翻掉了。学生们都觉得老师真是料事如神，问老师为什么能够猜测到车子会翻掉呢，老师说："我是从这件事的一种趋势中判断出来的。"几个学生急切地说："请老师讲给我们听听吧。"老师从容地回答："现在道路湿滑，唯独那高高的山路上勉强可以通过，可是那条山路又高又窄，天下着大雨，所有的车都往那边去，而那辆车子霸占在那里，还不顾别人着急，顽固地占据在高高的位置上，阻碍其他车子前进，它怎么能不翻掉呢?"学生们点头称是，佩服老师的判断正确。

接着，老师又语重心长地说："人的一生，就像一辆行驶的车子一样，会遭遇很多事情，一定要谦虚、谨慎，因为可能还会遇到比那车子翻掉更大的祸患。你们都要记住翻车的教训呀!"

While a teacher and several students went out to enjoy themselves, they ran into a heavy rain and it was hard for them to walk on the slippery road. On their way, they saw a carriage parked on a path high in the mountain. The teacher told the students, "Look. The carriage will soon be overturned." The students were surprised to hear that, so they asked, "Why?" The teacher answered, "Just wait and see." Then they kept walking.

Not long after, suddenly a loud noise burst from the road. They looked back and were surprised to find that the carriage had been turned over. The students now believed that their teacher really foretold things accurately, and asked the teacher why he could predict that. The teacher said, "I just judged from the tendency of this affair." Several students eagerly said, "Please tell us more." The teacher answered, "The road is wet and slippery, and the mountain road is barely passable for it is high and narrow. It rains heavily, and all the carriages have to go over there. But that carriage stays there regardless of other people's worry, occupying the road and hindering other carriages from moving forward. How can it not overturn?" The students couldn't help nodding their heads and admiring their teacher's judgment.

Then the teacher said to his students in earnest, "Our life is like a moving carriage which would encounter many things, so we must remain modest and prudent lest something more disastrous than overturning may happen. All of you should remember this lesson."

生难字/词注解 | Note

霸占：指仗势占为己有。

Occupy：Forcibly take things as one's own.

故事寓意 | The moral of the story

这个故事告诉我们：现实生活充满未知与偶然，要始终保持一种敬畏和谨慎的心态，踏实做事，谦逊做人。否则，一味地妄自尊大，目中无人，那将会很危险的。

This story tells us that life is full of unknown and accidental things. We should always be prudent，steadfast and humble. Otherwise，being blindly arrogant might cause dangers.

惧老休妻

Divorcing Wife in Fear of Aging Spouse

gǔ shí hou píng yuán jùn yí gè jiào táo qiū de rén qǔ le bó hǎi jùn
古时候，平原郡一个叫陶邱的人娶了渤海郡

mò tái shì de nǚ ér wéi qī zhè wèi nǚ zǐ bù jǐn róng mào měi lì ér
墨台氏的女儿为妻。这位女子不仅容貌美丽，而

qiě hěn yǒu cái huá wéi rén wēn róu xián shū hūn hòu táo qiū yì jiā guò zhe
且很有才华，为人温柔贤淑。婚后，陶邱一家过着

xìng fú měi mǎn de shēng huó suǒ yǒu de qīn qī lín jū dōu hěn xiàn mù táo
幸福美满的生活。所有的亲戚邻居都很羡慕陶

qiū yì nián hòu tā men shēng le gè ér zi jiā zhōng chōng mǎn le
邱。一年后，他们生了个儿子，家中充满了

huān xiào
欢笑。

yì tiān qī zi duì zhàng fu shuō jià dào nǐ jiā yǐ yǒu yì nián
一天，妻子对丈夫说："嫁到你家已有一年

了，这一年里我从没回过一次娘家，我很想念母亲，我们能不能回一趟娘家，顺便把孩子带给他们看看？"陶邱回答说："是呀，是应该去见见岳母了。"于是，陶邱一家三口选了个好日子，驾着马车来到了渤海郡。

娘家人见了女儿、女婿和小外孙，都非常高兴，杀鸡宰羊，把好吃好喝的都拿来招待他们。可是，岳母丁氏毕竟已经七十多岁了，她的脸上长满了皱纹，说话做事也不灵巧了，岳母才见过女婿之后，便觉得十分困乏，就回房间休息了。

几天后，陶邱带着妻子和儿子回家。一回到家就要和妻子离婚。妻子十分诧异，便问丈夫："我有什么过错呢？"陶邱说："前几天到你家去，见了你母亲。她的改变真让我伤心。她现在又老又丑，还没有一点待客的礼节。我担心你老了以后

yě huì biàn chéng zhè fù mú yàng dǎo bù rú xiàn zài lí hūn miǎn de yǐ hòu
也会变成这副模样，倒不如现在离婚，免得以后

rě wǒ shāng xīn   qī zi tīng tā zhè yàng shuō hěn shì wěi qū   kě shì tā
惹我伤心。"妻子听他这样说很是委屈，可是她

wú fǎ gǎi biàn zhàng fu de xiǎng fǎ   zhǐ děi dài zhe hái zi lí kāi le tā
无法改变丈夫的想法，只得带着孩子离开了他。

hòu lái   qīn qi hé lín jū zhī dào le zhè jiàn shì   dōu mà táo qiū tài
后来，亲戚和邻居知道了这件事，都骂陶邱太

yú chǔn tài kě xiào le   ér táo qiū jiù yīn wèi zhè yàng de xiǎo shì shī qù
愚蠢、太可笑了。而陶邱就因为这样的小事失去

le yí wèi xián dé de qī zi hé xìng fú de jiā tíng
了一位贤德的妻子和幸福的家庭。

Once upon a time, a guy named Tao Qiu from Pingyuan County married the daughter of Mr. Motai who resided in Bohai County. That girl has such uniqueness as beautiful countenance, great talent as well as virtues. After their wedding, the couple lived a harmonious life, and all their neighbors and relatives were jealous. A year later, they had a son, and laughter filled up every corner of their house.

One day, the wife said to her husband, "I have not been home since I married you. I really miss my mom desperately. Why don't we pay a visit to my mom with our son together?" Tao Qiu replied, "Yeah. It is time to meet my mother-in-law." Therefore, they chose a good day, starting their trip to Bohai County by carriage.

All the family members of the wife were very glad to see the daughter, son-in-law and their little grandson. They killed chickens and lambs, then cooked them to treat their guests with all their fabulous food and drinks. But after all, Madam Ding, his mother-in-law was over seventy, and her face was covered with wrinkles. She could not talk or behave as easily as she used to. After talking to Tao Qiu for a while, she felt already exhausted and went to her room to rest.

A few days later, Tao Qiu headed back home with his wife and son. He told his intention of divorcing his wife as he trod on the threshold. And his wife was so astounded that she questioned, "What should I be blamed for?" Tao Qiu replied, "After seeing your mother several days ago, I was quite upset by your mother's changes. She looked so old and ugly. Besides, she behaved badly to her guests. I'm worrying that you will be like your mother when you get old. It's better to divorce now, so as not to upset me in the future." Hearing what her husband said, she felt depressed but had no chance to change his mind. She had to leave with her son.

After knowing that news, all relatives and neighbors scolded him for being too stupid and ridiculous. Just for such a trivial excuse, Tao Qiu lost a virtuous wife and a happy family forever.

故事寓意 | The moral of the story

这位丈夫因担心妻子变老变丑而放弃美好的婚姻,是很愚蠢的做法。因为生老病死是每个人都不可能避免的自然规律。这个故事告诉我们:不论做什么都要不忘初心,从一而终,不负真爱,懂得珍惜,只有这样才能拥有幸福和快乐。

It is foolish for the husband to give up a good marriage because of the fear that his wife may become old and ugly. Birth, aging, sickness and death are the most natural things in our lives. This story tells us that no matter what to do, we should not forget our original intention, and we should be loyal to our true love and cherish it, thus we can have happiness and joy.

山鸡与凤凰

The Pheasant and the Phoenix

yí gè chǔ guó rén wài chū de shí hou　pèng dào yí gè tiāo zhe shān jī
一个楚国人外出的时候，碰到一个挑着山鸡

de nóng fū　zhè gè chǔ guó rén cóng lái méi yǒu jiàn guò shān jī　suǒ yǐ
的农夫。这个楚国人从来没有见过山鸡。所以，

dāng tā kàn dào zhè zhī shān jī zhǎng zhe piào liang yǔ máo hé xiū cháng wěi ba
当他看到这只山鸡长着漂亮羽毛和修长尾巴

de shí hou　hěn hào qí de wèn　nǐ tiāo de shì yì zhī shén me niǎo　nà
的时候，很好奇地问："你挑的是一只什么鸟？"那

nóng fū jiàn tā bú rèn shi shān jī　biàn méng piàn tā shuō　zhè shì yì zhī
农夫见他不认识山鸡，便蒙骗他说："这是一只

fèng huáng　zhè ge chǔ guó rén tīng le shí fēn gāo xìng　biàn xìng fèn de shuō
凤凰。"这个楚国人听了十分高兴，便兴奋地说

dào　wǒ yǐ qián zhǐ shì tīng shuō yǒu fèng huáng　jīn tiān zhōng yú jiàn dào le
道："我以前只是听说有凤凰，今天终于见到了

fèng huáng　nǐ néng bu néng bǎ tā mài gěi wǒ　nóng fū shuō　kě
凤凰！你能不能把它卖给我？"农夫说："可

以。"这个楚国人出价十两黄金。那农夫想："既然这个傻瓜把山鸡当成凤凰,我为什么不趁此机会抬高价钱呢?"于是,他把价格提高了一倍。

这个楚国人还是很高兴地把山鸡买回家去了,并打算第二天去敬献给楚王。

可是没有意料到过了一夜,山鸡却死了。这个楚国人看着那只没有一点气息,已经僵硬的山鸡,非常伤心。他不是可惜自己付出的钱财,而是心痛没有能够将"凤凰"这种吉祥物敬献给楚王。

这件事情被很多人传说,很快楚王也知道了。楚王虽然没有得到凤凰,但是被这个人的忠心感动。楚王派侍卫把这个楚国人传召到宫中,赏赐给了他比买山鸡付出的价钱还多十倍的金子。

When a man from the State of Chu went out, he encountered a farmer carrying a pheasant which he had never seen. He was curious to see the pheasant with beautiful feathers and a slender tail, so he asked, "What kind of bird are you carrying?" The farmer found that he could not recognize the pheasant, so he lied to him, "This is a phoenix." The man from the State of Chu was very excited, thus he said, "I've only heard of phoenix, and today finally I have the chance to meet it. Would you like to sell it to me?" The farmer answered, "OK." The man from the State of Chu made a bid of ten taels of gold, but the farmer thought, "Since this fool regarded the pheasant as phoenix, why don't I take advantage of this opportunity to raise the price?" So he doubled the price. The man was still happy to buy the pheasant and took it back home. He decided to present it to the king of the State of Chu the next day.

But unexpectedly, the pheasant died overnight. The man from the State of Chu watched the stiff pheasant and felt very sad. He was not feeling pity for the money he paid for the pheasant, but for not being able to present the auspicious "phoenix" to the king.

The story was told from people to people, and soon the king of the State of Chu also knew it. Though the king didn't get the phoenix, he was moved by the man's loyalty. Therefore, the king summoned the man into the palace, and bestowed upon him gold ten times more than that he had paid for the pheasant.

故事寓意 | The moral of the story

这个故事告诉我们：忠厚老实的人有的时候会吃亏上当，但是，却更加能够得到认可与尊重。而那些行骗的人终有一天会受到良心的谴责。

This story tells us that honest people sometimes may get fooled, but they are more likely to get recognition and respect for this virtue. Meanwhile, those who cheat will eventually feel the pricks of conscience.

守株待兔

To Stand by a Tree Stump Waiting for a Hare

春秋时期，宋国有个农夫，每天在田地里劳动。一天，他正在地里干活，突然一只野兔从草丛中蹿出来，恰巧撞在树桩上，脖子被折断，野兔死了。农夫放下手中的农具，走过去捡起死兔子。他非常庆幸自己的好运气，他想，要是每天都能捡到野兔，就不用辛辛苦苦地种地了。

dì èr tiān tā dào dì lǐ gàn huó zài yě bú xiàng yǐ qián nà me zhuān xīn
第二天，他到地里干活再也不像以前那么专心

le tā xī wàng hái yǒu yì zhī tù zi néng gòu zhuàng sǐ zài shù zhuāng shang
了。他希望还有一只兔子能够撞死在树桩上，

kě shì zhí dào tiān hēi yě méi yǒu jiàn dào yǒu tù zi chū lái tā hěn bù gān xīn
可是，直到天黑也没有见到有兔子出来,他很不甘心

de huí jiā le dì sān tiān nóng fū yǐ jīng wán quán méi yǒu xīn sī chú dì
地回家了。第三天，农夫已经完全没有心思锄地

le tā bǎ nóng jù fàng zài yì biān zhuān mén zuò zài shù zhuāng páng biān děng
了,他把农具放在一边，专门坐在树桩旁边等

dài tù zi pǎo guò lái kě shì nǎ yǒu zhè me hǎo de pián yi jiǎn ne jié
待兔子跑过来。可是哪有这么好的便宜捡呢。结

guǒ děng le yì tiān shén me yě méi děng dào tā què bù gān xīn
果，等了一天什么也没等到,他却不甘心。

cóng cǐ tā tiān tiān zuò zài nà kē dà shù xià děng zhe tù zi de dào
从此,他天天坐在那棵大树下等着兔子的到

lái tā děng ya děng ya děng dào dì lǐ de yě cǎo zhǎng de bǐ zhuāng
来。他等呀等呀，等到地里的野草长得比庄

jia dōu gāo le lián gè yě tù yǐng zi yě méi yǒu zài jiàn dao
稼都高了,连个野兔影子也没有再见到。

During the Spring and Autumn period，there was a farmer in
the State of Song who worked in the fields every day. One day，
while he was working in the fields，suddenly a hare from the grass
bumped against the stump，broke its neck and died. The farmer

stopped his work and went to pick up the dead hare. He was overjoyed at his good luck, and he thought he would not need to work so hard if he could catch a hare every day.

The next day, he did not work as hard as before and just wished another hare to dash against the stump. But still no hare appeared until it was dark, and he returned home disappointedly. The third day, the farmer had no mood to do farming work at all. He put his tools aside, sitting beside the stump and waiting for more hares to dash against the stump. How could he be so lucky? He waited the whole day but no hare came. He was so unsatisfied.

Since then, he sat under the tree every day, waiting for the hares. He kept waiting and waiting, but till the weeds in the field grew taller than the crops, no hares had ever shown again.

故事寓意 | The moral of the story

"守株待兔"比喻不想努力却希望获得成功的侥幸心理。这个故事告诉我们：不要抱着不劳而获的侥幸心理，要脚踏实地地努力耕耘，才会有丰硕的果实。

"To stand by a tree stump waiting for a hare" describes people's fluky idea that they would succeed without making efforts. The story tells us that we should not expect that we may reap without sowing. Instead, we should work hard and make great efforts in order to win what we want.

塞翁失马

A Blessing in Disguise

从前，边塞上有个老人，性情爽朗、豁达。

一天，老人家走失了一匹马，邻居们知道了，担心他过于悲伤，特地过来安慰他，可是老人却觉得没有什么要紧，他反而劝慰邻居："丢失了马本来是一件坏事，但谁知道它会不会变成一件好事呢？"

过了几个月，那匹丢失的马跑回来了，并且还带回了一匹骏马。邻居们听说后，又来向老人贺喜，老人却说："唉，多了一匹马本来是件好事，可谁知道这件事会不会变成灾祸呢？"老人家多了

zhè pǐ jùn mǎ hòu   tā de ér zi gāo xìng jí le   zhěng tiān qí zhe mǎ chū qù
这匹骏马后，他的儿子高兴极了，整天骑着马出去

wán shuǎ   yì tiān   lǎo rén de ér zi bù xiǎo xīn cóng mǎ bèi shang diào le
玩耍。一天，老人的儿子不小心从马背上掉了

xià lái   shuāi duàn le yì tiáo tuǐ   lín jū men tīng dào hòu   gǎn jǐn lái wèi
下来，摔断了一条腿。邻居们听到后，赶紧来慰

wèn   lǎo rén yòu shuō   shuāi shāng le shì jiàn huài shì   shéi zhī dào tā huì
问。老人又说："摔伤了是件坏事，谁知道它会

bu huì dài lái hǎo de jié guǒ ne
不会带来好的结果呢？"

guò le yì nián   biān jìng fā shēng zhàn zhēng   shēn qiáng lì zhuàng de
过了一年，边境发生战争，身强力壮的

nián qīng rén dōu bèi zhēng qù dǎ zhàng   dà bù fen rén dōu sǐ le   ér lǎo
年轻人都被征去打仗，大部分人都死了。而老

rén de ér zi yīn wèi shì gè bǒ tuǐ   méi yǒu zhēng qù dǎ zhàng   zuì zhōng dé
人的儿子因为是个跛腿，没有征去打仗，最终得

yǐ bǎo quán xìng mìng
以保全性命。

Once upon a time, there was an open-minded and optimistic old man living near the frontier fortress. One day, one of the old man's horses ran away and got lost, and his neighbors all came to console him. But the old man was not sad at all, comforting his neighbors instead, "Losing a horse is a bad thing, but how do we know it wouldn't become a good thing?"

After a few months, the lost horse came back, followed by another fine horse. After hearing this, the neighbors came to congratulate him. However, the old man said unexpectedly, "Alas, it is a good thing to have one more horse, but nobody knows it wouldn't turn out to be a disaster." The old man's son was extremely excited for the new fine horse and rode it all day long. One day, his son fell from the back of the horse and broke one leg. His neighbors again came to comfort him. The old man said, "Breaking a leg is a bad thing, but maybe it would bring good result."

One year later, all the young people were recruited to fight in the war near the frontier fortress, and most of them died. The old man's son was not required to join the army because of his broken leg, and thus saved his life.

故事寓意 | The moral of the story

"塞翁失马"用来比喻人世间的事情都是相对的,在一定条件下会相互转换。这个故事告诉我们:要从容、淡定地去面对一切发生的事情,用辩证的眼光看待人生祸福。

"A blessing in disguise" informs us that good and bad points of one situation are closely connected, and under some conditions they would change into each other. The story tells us that we should face everything calmly and treat disastrous and lucky things with a dialectical view.

亡羊补牢

Mending the Fold After a Sheep Is Lost

从前有一个牧民，养了几十只羊。他白天放羊，晚上就把羊赶进一个用柴草和木桩等物围起来的羊圈内。

一天早晨，这个牧民去放羊，发现羊少了一只。他很惊讶，就去查看羊圈，才发现不知道什么时候羊圈破了个窟窿，有狼趁着晚上天黑从那个窟窿里钻了进去，把一只羊叼走了。邻居听

说 这 件 事 情 后 ，都 替 他 着 急 ，就 劝 告 他 说："赶 快
把 羊 圈 修 一 修 ，堵 上 那 个 窟 窿 吧 。"他 不 急 不 躁 地
说："羊 已 经 丢 了 ，还 去 修 羊 圈 干 什 么 呢 ？"他 没
有 听 从 邻 居 的 劝 告 。

第 二 天 早 上 ，他 去 放 羊 ，发 现 羊 又 少 了 一
只 。 原 来 狼 又 从 窟 窿 里 钻 进 羊 圈 ，叼 走 了 一 只
羊 。 这 时 他 才 后 悔 没 有 听 从 邻 居 的 劝 告 。 于 是 ，
他 赶 紧 堵 塞 住 那 个 窟 窿 ，把 羊 圈 进 行 一 番 加 固 ，修
得 十 分 结 实 。

从 此 ，这 个 牧 民 的 羊 就 再 也 没 有 被 野 狼 叼 走 过 。

There was once a farmer who raised scores of sheep. He herded the sheep into a pasture to graze in the daytime，and in the evening he drove the sheep into a sheepfold built of wood piles and hay.

One morning, the man found a sheep missing, so he checked the sheepfold and found a hole in it. It turned out that wolves sneaked into the sheepfold through the hole and carried one sheep away. After hearing this, his neighbor gave him a piece of advice, "You should mend the sheepfold and fill in the hole at once." But he answered, "The sheep is already gone, so why bother to mend the sheepfold?" He didn't take the advice.

The second day, he woke up early and found one more sheep missing. It turned out that wolves again sneaked into the sheepfold through the hole and carried one sheep away. Until then he felt regretful for not having taken the advice. He soon reinforced the sheepfold and filled the hole.

Ever since then, no sheep had been taken by wild wolves.

生难字/词注解 | Note

窟窿：在物体内部的空洞或孔隙。

Hole：Gap inside an object.

故事寓意 | The moral of the story

"亡羊补牢"用来比喻受到损失后，及时想办法补救，以避免更大的损失。这个故事告诉我们：遭遇挫折失败并不可怕，只要能够认真吸取教训，及时采取措施，就可以避免遭受更大的灾祸。

"Mending the fold after a sheep is lost" is used to describe the situation that people take remedial action after damage in order to avoid greater loss. This story tells us that failure is not terrible, and as long as you can draw a lesson and take measures in time, you can avoid suffering from greater disaster.

无价之宝

The Invaluable Treasure

yǒu yì tiān   xī yù lái le yí gè shāng rén   zài jí shì shang chū shòu
有一天，西域来了一个商人，在集市上出售

zhū bǎo   zhè xiē zhū bǎo guāng cǎi duó mù   jià gé áng guì   lǐ miàn zuì hǎo
珠宝。这些珠宝光彩夺目，价格昂贵。里面最好

de shì yì kē míng jiào shān de bǎo zhū   tā yán sè chì hóng tōng tòu   zhí
的是一颗名叫"珊"的宝珠，它颜色赤红通透，直

jìng zú yǒu yí cùn   jià zhí gāo dá bǎi wàn   zhè kē bǎo zhū xī yǐn le xǔ duō
径足有一寸，价值高达百万。这颗宝珠吸引了许多

rén zhù zú wéi guān   dà jiā dōu yì kǒu tóng shēng de zàn tàn dào   zhè kě
人驻足围观，大家都异口同声地赞叹道："这可

zhēn shì shì jiān shǎo yǒu de bǎo bèi a
真是世间少有的宝贝啊！"

lóng mén zǐ bó xué duō shí   qià hǎo zhè tiān tā yě lái guàng jiē
龙门子博学多识，恰好这天他也来逛街。

他见这么多人围在一起看热闹，就走上前去。

龙门子看着宝珠，问道："珊可以用来填饱肚子吗？"商人回答说："不行。"龙门子又问："那它可以治病吗？"商人又回答说："不行。"龙门子接着问："那它能够驱除灾祸吗？"商人回答："不能。""那能使人更加孝顺吗？"商人的回答还是"不能"。龙门子说道："真是奇怪，这颗珠子没有什么用，却价值连城，这是为什么呢？"商人回答说："这是因为珊出产在很遥远的地方，要想得到它必须动用大量的人力物力，历经艰难险阻才能得到它。这可是非常稀罕的宝贝啊！"龙门子听了，笑了笑，什么也没说便离开了。

龙门子有一个学生，名叫郑渊。他听到老师与商人的谈话后，很是疑惑。便问老师为何人们争相抢夺的珠宝在他眼里却一文不值。龙门子便教导他说："古人曾经说过，黄金虽然是宝贝，但是人若吞吃了它，便会死亡；它的粉末若掉进了人的眼睛里，也会致瞎。我已经很久不去追求这些东西了。从表面上来看我一无所有，但是从内里来看我身上也有贵重的宝贝，它的价值绝对不止数百万。而且水淹没不了它，火烧毁不了它，风吹日晒也无法损坏它。用它可以使天下安定；不用它则可以使我安然舒坦。人们不去追求这样的至宝，反倒把寻求珠宝当作此生最为要紧的事，这岂不是舍近求远、愚不可及吗？唉，看来人心已死了很久了！"

One day, there came a merchant from the Western Regions who sold jewelries which were radiant with shining brightness and labeled at high prices. Among all these jewelries, one precious bead called Shan was the best which was transparent in a color of scarlet. With its diameter measured one inch, it was valued at nearly a million. That precious bead drew so much attention from people who walked by that they stopped to circle around and appreciate it. Everyone who saw it gave compliments to this bead unanimously with amazement, "It is such a valuable treasure in the world."

Longmenzi, a man with rich knowledge and experience, happened to be hanging out around the market that day. He saw many people circled together watching something, then he went forward and saw this bead, questioning, "Can it feed our stomach?"The merchant said no. "Can it cure illness?" Again the merchant said no. He continued, "Can it drive away natural disasters or bad luck?" It was a no still. "Can it make people more filial?" The answer was the same. Longmenzi asked again with confusion, "It is so strange that it is worth millions but yet there is nothing useful." "Because it was produced afar, and it takes so much labor and resource to get it. It is a rarity for much painstaking efforts are needed to find this treasure." After hearing such an answer, Longmenzi did not say anything but left with a smile.

Zheng Yuan, one of Longmenzi's students, felt quite perplexed when he heard the conversation between his teacher and the merchant. So he asked Longmenzi why the jewelry which everyone struggled to obtain seemed worthless to him. Longmenzi then instructed him, "There is a saying goes like that: 'Though gold is precious, we eat it, we die; if its powder falls into eyes, we will turn blind.' It has been for a while that it is not my pursuit anymore.

It appears that I have nothing，but actually I have precious fortune in my inner world. And its worth is absolutely far more than millions. The water cannot drown it，the fire cannot burn it，nor can the wind and sun. If I use it，the world can enjoy peace. Even if I don't use it，I can get comfort and peace in my heart. Isn't it stupid as people seek precious objects while neglecting invaluable spiritual fortune that lies in our hearts? Ah，people's hearts died long ago."

故事寓意 | **The moral of the story**

龙门子所说的"至宝",指的是人们身上所拥有的美德。这个故事告诉我们：只有高尚的道德品质、纯净的心灵和仁慈的胸怀才是人一生中最大的财富。只有这些高贵的品行才是值得人们终生去追求的无价之宝。

The "invaluable treasure" mentioned by Longmenzi refers to our virtues. This story tells us that noble moralities, a pure heart and a benevolent mind are the greatest wealth in our life. Only these noble qualities are worth pursuing throughout our life.

终身不遇

Dream Unrealized All Lifetime

cóng qián　　luò yáng yǒu yí　gè　dú shū rén　　tā　bì shēng de mèng xiǎng
从 前，洛 阳 有 一 个 读 书 人，他 毕 生 的 梦 想

jiù shì zuò guān　　kě shì　　yì zhí dào tā nián jì dà le　　yě méi yǒu móu dé
就 是 做 官 。可 是，一 直 到 他 年 纪 大 了，也 没 有 谋 得

yì guān bàn zhí　　zhè ràng tā shí fēn bēi shāng
一 官 半 职，这 让 他 十 分 悲 伤 。

yì tiān　tā zǒu zài lù shang　　xiǎng dào zì jǐ　yǐ jīng lǎo qù　què yī rán
一 天，他 走 在 路 上 ，想 到 自 己 已 经 老 去，却 依 然

yí shì wú chéng　bù jīn liú xià le shāng xīn de yǎn lèi　　yǒu rén gǎn dào hěn
一 事 无 成，不 禁 流 下 了 伤 心 的 眼 泪 。有 人 感 到 很

qí guài　jiù wèn tā　　lǎo rén jia　qǐng wèn nín wèi shén me shāng xīn ne　　zhè
奇 怪，就 问 他："老 人 家，请 问 您 为 什 么 伤 心 呢?"这

个人回答说："我想做官想了一辈子,可上天却始终没有给我机会。眼看自己就这样老去,我这一辈子都不可能有做官的机会了。我这一生就这么一个梦想都没有实现,所以我怎能不伤心啊!"

年轻人又说："那么多求官的人都得到了官职,你为什么却一次机会也没遇上呢?"这个老人回答说："我年轻的时候学的是文科,等到我在这方面学有所成出来求官时,遇到的皇帝恰好喜欢提拔经验丰富的老年人。我就这样白白错失了一次机会。很多年后,那个喜欢任用老年人的君主驾崩了,我又出来求官。本以为此次定能成功,可谁知继承王位的皇帝却是个喜爱武士的人,我又一次失去了机会。为了能够成为朝廷官员,我放弃学文而去钻研武艺。可等我刚学好武艺时,那个重视武艺的君主也驾崩了。现

zài jì chéng wáng wèi de shì yí wèi nián qīng de jūn zhǔ tīng shuō tā xǐ huān
在继承王位的是一位年轻的君主，听说他喜欢

tí bá nián qīng rén zuò guān ér wǒ zǎo yǐ bú zài nián qīng le gēn běn jiù
提拔年轻人做官。而我早已不再年轻了，根本就

bù kě néng yǒu bèi tí bá de jī huì wǒ zhè yí bèi zi shēng bù féng shí
不可能有被提拔的机会。我这一辈子生不逢时，

méi yǒu yù dào yí cì zuò guān de jī huì zhè nán dào bú shì jiàn shí fēn kě
没有遇到一次做官的机会，这难道不是件十分可

bēi de shì ma shuō wán tā yòu jīn bú zhù shī shēng tòng kū qǐ lái
悲的事吗？"说完，他又禁不住失声痛哭起来。

Once, there in the city of Luoyang lived a scholar who pinned his great hopes on being an official. Nevertheless, he wasn't appointed to any post in the court through his whole life, which made him very upset.

One day, plodding on the way, he couldn't help shedding sorrowful tears at the thought of his aging without any achievement. Someone felt fairly strange toward this, hence asked him, "Hey, you, old fellow, why are you so sad?" The man answered, "I have always been craving for securing an official post for a lifetime. But god didn't endow me with an opportunity all the time. Now I'm on the path to decease and I can't make it come true in this life. I merely have one dream this life but it remains unrealized. How can I not feel upset?"

The young man inquired again, "Many people in pursuit of a post in the court have made it, and how come you couldn't seize a single opportunity?" The old man thus claimed, "I learned liberal arts while young. But when I've made some achievements in the field to pursue an official post, the emperor happened to have a great favor for promoting some experienced elderly, hence an opportunity was lost. Many years later, the old emperor died and I came back to apply for a post once again. I thought I could hit a success this time but who can predict that the successor was particularly fond of warriors, hence another opportunity elapsed. In order to be an official, I temporarily changed my mind to give up on liberal arts and undertook skills in martial arts. However, the moment I acquired it, the emperor passed away. Later on, I got the news that the new young emperor liked to promote the young. I was no longer young, hence the deprivation of my opportunity to be promoted. I wasn't born into the appropriate time, therefore, I couldn't be endowed with an opportunity to serve in the court. Doesn't it sound pathetic?" After this explanation, he couldn't help crying in a loud voice.

故事寓意 | The moral of the story

这个故事告诉我们：一旦确定了某个目标，就要脚踏实地、矢志不渝地去努力奋斗，总有一天成功的机遇会降临到我们头上。如果我们像文中的老人那样，一经历挫折就改变志向，那这一生也只能碌碌无为，沦为平庸。

This story informs us that once we set a goal, we should stick to it and fight for it insistently. Eventually the opportunity of success would befall on us. If we behave like the old man in the story who changes his aim once confronted with obstacles, we would definitely achieve nothing but reduce to be mediocre the whole lifetime.

钻牛角尖

Taking Unnecessary Pains to Study an Insignificant Problem

yǒu yí gè dú shū rén　xué shí hěn dī qiǎn　kě shì bù guǎn yù dào
有一个读书人，学识很低浅，可是不管遇到

shén me wèn tí dōu xǐ huān yǔ rén jì jiào　zhēng lùn bù xiū　tīng shuō ài
什么问题都喜欢与人计较，争论不休。听说艾

zǐ xué fù wǔ chē　wéi rén hé shàn　zhè ge dú shū rén jiù xiǎng diāo nàn
子学富五车，为人和善，这个读书人就想刁难

ài zǐ
艾子。

yì tiān　tā zhuān chéng qù bài fǎng ài zǐ　wèn dào　dà chē de chē
一天，他专程去拜访艾子，问道："大车的车

shēn xià miàn hé luò tuo de bó zi shang　dōu jì zhe líng dang　zhè shì wèi shén
身下面和骆驼的脖子上，都系着铃铛，这是为什

me ne　ài zǐ huí dá shuō　dà chē hé luò tuo dōu shì hěn dà de　gěi
么呢？"艾子回答说："大车和骆驼都是很大的，给

tā men guà shàng líng dang shì wèi le　bì miǎn tā men zài yè jiān gǎn lù shí
它们挂上铃铛是为了避免它们在夜间赶路时

相互碰撞。"那人接着又问:"佛塔的顶端也挂

着铃铛,难道佛塔也需要避免和其他物体相撞

吗?"艾子说:"你这个人真是呆板呀。你知道那

些鸟雀喜欢在高处筑巢,在塔上挂着铃铛是为

了避免鸟雀在高塔上筑巢呀。"见艾子轻而易举

地解答了这个问题,那个人心里很不是滋味。他又

继续问道:"猎鹰、鹞子的尾巴上也都带着小铃

铛,这也是为了防止鸟雀在它们的尾巴上筑

巢吗?"

艾子听了,忍不住笑了起来,说:"看你也是个

读书人,是故意装傻呢还是真不开窍呀?猎鹰、

鹞子捕捉鸟兽常常进入灌木丛中,束脚的

绳子有时会被树枝缠绕,鸟儿振动翅膀时铃

声就会响起来,猎人听到铃声就会赶过去救它

们呀!"读书人继续问艾子:"我见过那送葬的队

伍，前面有个人总是摇着铃铛唱挽歌。现在才知道原来是怕树枝缠住他的脚，以便让人们找到他呀。只是我还想问您，那个人脚上的带子是用皮条做的呢，还是用丝线编成的呢？"

艾子实在不耐烦了，生气地回答："那个摇铃铛的人是死者的向导，因为这死者活着的时候喜欢与人计较，故意习难人，所以才摇着铃铛让他的尸体感到快乐呀！"

那个读书人听了，知道自己的意图被识破，只好羞愧地走开了。

Once there was a scholar with little talent and learning, but he liked arguing with others on whatever problems. When he heard that Aizi was versatile and friendly with people, the scholar decided to make him feel embarrassed.

One day, he purposely came to visit Aizi to ask him why there was a small bell under the cart body and on the camel's neck. Aizi answered, "The cart and the camel are very large, so hanging a bell would prevent them from hitting other carts and camels when they hurry on with their journey at night." Then the scholar continued asking, "There is a bell on the top of the pagoda. Does that mean the pagodas also need to avoid crashing into other objects?" Aizi said, "You are really inflexible. You know, birds like to make nests at high places. So, hanging a bell on the top of a pagoda is to prevent the birds' nesting." The scholar felt jealous and bitter when he found that Aizi could answer these questions so easily. He did not give up and went on asking, "There are also small bells on falcon's and sparrow hawk's tails. Is that for stopping birds' nesting too?"

Aizi couldn't help laughing, and he said, "You are also a scholar. Are you kidding me or are you a real hard nut? The falcons and sparrow hawks always go into bushes to catch birds, and sometimes the ropes around their feet will be winded by branches. The bell will ring when they shake their wings, and then the hunter can go to save them as soon as he hears the sound. The scholar continued to ask Aizi, "I have seen a funeral procession that the leading person is always shaking a bell and singing dirge. Today I finally know that he is afraid of branches to wind his feet. He does so for people to find and help him. But are the belts on that person's feet made by strap or silk ribbon?"

Aizi felt annoyed and became impatient, and he answered angrily, "The person who shakes the bell is the guide of the dead man. The dead used to haggle with others and make things difficult for others on purpose when he was alive. So people shake the bell to make the corpse happy."

When the scholar heard this, he knew that his trick had been seen through. Then he went away in dejection.

生难字/词注解 | Note

呆板：死板，不自然，不灵活。
Inflexible：Dull.

故事寓意 | The moral of the story

"钻牛角尖"用来比喻费力去做或思考无法解决或不值得的事情；也指思想狭隘、偏执。这个故事告诉我们：人要有自知之明，懂得进退。如果钻入"牛角尖"，结果往往是自讨苦吃。

"Taking unnecessary pains to study an insignificant problem" is used to describe that people take pains to do or try to solve unanswerable problems. It's also used to depict people who are narrow-minded or paranoid. The story informs us that we should know our own limitations and when to stop. If we take unnecessary pains to study the insignificant problem, we will get frustrated in the end.

纸上谈兵

To Fight Only on Paper

战国时期，赵国的著名将领赵奢有一个儿子，名叫赵括。赵括从小熟读兵书，谈论兵法的时候总是头头是道，连他父亲都辩驳不了他。但是，他父亲却了解赵括只知道背诵兵书，难以担当重任。

一次，秦国攻打赵国。赵国一开始派遣老将廉颇作为统帅，廉颇依据战争情形，下令让军队坚守阵地，以保存实力拖垮秦军。秦军渐渐粮食短缺，十分恐慌。于是秦国施展离间计，在赵国上下散布谣言，说："秦军谁都不怕，就怕赵括担任大将。"这个时候，由于赵王不满意廉颇的保守战法，又听到外面流传谣言，于是赵王撤掉廉颇，委派赵括为大将。

赵括率领四十万大军去攻打秦军，先是大量撤换将官，导致赵军上下人心惶惶。接着，在与秦军交战的时候，指挥失当，轻率行事，结果中了秦军设下的埋伏，导致了全军覆没，他自己也被乱箭射死。赵国从此以后没落了。

During the Warring States period, in the State of Zhao, the famous general Zhao She had a son named Zhao Kuo who was familiar with books about the art of war. When Zhao Kuo talked about military tactics eloquently, even his father couldn't dispute with him. But his father knew that he could just recite military books but was not able to take command.

Once, the State of Qin attacked the State of Zhao. The veteran general Lian Po was appointed as commander in chief, and according to the situation, he ordered the troops to maintain their formation in order to preserve their strength and exhaust the Qin's army. Gradually, Qin's troop panicked for being short of food, so they played the scheme of sowing dissension. They spread the rumor around the State of Zhao, "Qin is not afraid of anything but Zhao Kuo being general." At that time, King of Zhao was not satisfied with Lian Po's conservative strategy, so he replaced Lian Po with Zhao Kuo after he heard the rumor.

Zhao Kuo led the troop of over four hundred thousand soldiers to fight against Qin's army. First he dismissed and replaced lots of officers, but this caused great worry in the army. In the following battle, because of his faulty direction and reckless action, they were beguiled into ambush. The whole army was defeated and Zhao Kuo himself was shot to death. Since then, the State of Zhao began to decline.

故事寓意 | The moral of the story

"纸上谈兵"用来形容那些没有实践经验只会夸夸其谈的人。这个故事告诉我们：实践出真知，要有真才实学，除了学习理论知识之外，还要勤于在实践中运用理论，检验真理。

"To fight only on paper" is used to describe those who just talk about the theory with no practical experience. This story tells us that genuine knowledge could only be gained through practicing, and to master solid knowledge, we should not only learn theories, but also practice and test them.

中　国　经　典　寓　言　故　事

第三辑

Part 3

伯愁和千里马

Bochou and Swift Horses

bó chóu hé bó lè cóng xiǎo jiù shì hěn hǎo de péng you bó chóu
伯愁和伯乐从小就是很好的朋友。伯愁

zhǎng dà hòu gěi bié rén mò miàn wéi chí shēng huó rì zi guò de hěn pín
长大后，给别人磨面维持生活，日子过得很贫

kǔ wèi cǐ tā zhěng tiān dōu hěn fán nǎo
苦。为此他整天都很烦恼。

yì tiān tā qù le yí tàng chéng lǐ huí dào jiā hòu shí fēn kāi xīn
一天，他去了一趟城里，回到家后，十分开心。

tā xiào mī mī de duì qī zi shuō jīn tiān wǒ zài chéng lǐ yù jiàn wǒ de
他笑眯眯地对妻子说："今天我在城里遇见我的

hǎo péng you bó lè la tā dā ying sòng wǒ yì pǐ qiān lǐ mǎ qiān lǐ mǎ
好朋友伯乐啦，他答应送我一匹千里马！千里马

yì tiān kě xíng zǒu qiān lǐ jí biàn shì zài wǎn shang zuì shǎo yě néng zǒu bā
一天可行走千里，即便是在晚上，最少也能走八

bǎi lǐ nǐ suàn yi suàn rú guǒ wǒ men yòng qiān lǐ mǎ lái mò miàn yì
百里。你算一算，如果我们用千里马来磨面，一

天能磨多少面呀！以后，咱们的生活就不用发愁了！"妻子曾经听别人说过，伯乐很善于辨识千里马，现在听丈夫这么一说，她心里也十分高兴。

第二天早上，伯愁把家里那匹拉磨的黑马牵到城里去卖掉。中午，他骑着一匹枣红色的马回来了。这匹马浑身毛发油亮，像披了一层光滑的绸缎似的。伯愁高兴地对妻子说："这是匹千里追风赤兔马，我骑着它从城里回来，足足百里路，花了不到一个小时！"接下来的日子，伯愁用这匹赤兔马来拉磨碾面。可是很奇怪，这匹赤兔马走得比那匹黑马还慢。因此，伯愁的生活并没有得到改善，他又重新陷入了愁苦当中，整天唉声叹气。他说："唉！大家都说伯乐很善于辨识千里马，我看他也只是徒有虚名罢了！"

guò le yí duàn shí jiān yǒu lín jū dào chéng lǐ qù lín jū huí lái hòu
过了一段时间，有邻居到城里去。邻居回来后

duì bó chóu shuō tā zài jí shì shang kàn dào bó lè yòu fā xiàn le yì pǐ qiān lǐ
对伯愁说，他在集市上看到伯乐又发现了一匹千里

wū zhuī mǎ zhè pǐ wū zhuī mǎ jiù shì bó chóu jiā yuán lái nà pǐ lā mò de hēi
乌骓马。这匹乌骓马，就是伯愁家原来那匹拉磨的黑

mǎ bó chóu tīng le xīn lǐ shí fēn ào nǎo bù kěn xiāng xìn zhè shì zhēn de
马。伯愁听了，心里十分懊恼，不肯相信这是真的。

tā yí gè jìnr de yáo tóu shuō xiào hua zhè gēn běn bù kě néng ya
他一个劲儿地摇头，说："笑话，这根本不可能呀！"

Bochou and Bole were good friends since they were young. When Bochou grew up, he made a living by grinding flour but could hardly make both ends meet. Therefore, he had a hard life and kept a bitter look all the time.

One day, he came back from the town and was very happy. He said to his wife smilingly, "Today I met my good friend Bole in the town, and he promised to send me a swift horse. The horse could walk a thousand *li* a day and even eight hundred *li* one night. Just think about it. If we make the horse grind the flour, how much flour it can grind! In the future, there is no doubt that our life would turn much better." The wife had already heard that Bole did well in searching swift horses, so she also felt delighted when her husband told her this.

The day after, in the early morning, Bochou brought his black horse which did the grinding job to the market and sold it. At noon, he came back by riding a purplish red horse with shiny fur as smooth as silk. He said excitedly to his wife, "This is an excellent swift horse. I rode it back from town for a hundred *li* within just one hour!" In the following days, Bochou made the horse grind, but strangely it walked even slower than his former black horse. Hence, Bochou's living had not been improved at all, and he again felt unhappy, sighing always. He said, "Well! People all say that Bole is good at finding swift horses, but I think he is enjoying undeserved fame."

After a while, one of his neighbors went to the town. When he returned, he told Bochou that he saw Bole find another swift dark horse which was the one that did grinding job in Bochou's home. Bochou felt chagrined and couldn't believe it. He shook his head and said, "Nonsense. It's impossible."

故事寓意 | The moral of the story

伯乐是春秋时期的人,对马非常有研究,善于相马。民间传说"世有伯乐,然后有千里马。"是说只有伯乐,千里马才能被发现、被赏识。如果没有伯乐,千里马的才能也许被埋没了,最后沦为平庸之辈。这个故事告诉我们:不仅要具备才华,还需要一个能够欣赏你才华的人,只有这样,我们才能更容易接近成功。

Bole lived in the Spring and Autumn period, and he was good at identifying and choosing swift horses. There is a saying goes like "Where there is Bole, there is the swift horse." That is to say the swift horses can just be recognized and appreciated by Bole. Without Bole, the gift of a swift horse may be neglected and it may become an ordinary horse. The story tells us that we should not only be equipped with talent, but also need someone who would recognize and appreciate our ability, and only in this way, can we get closer to success.

管中窥豹

To See Only One Spot of Leopard Through a Pipe

晋代著名书法家王羲之有一个儿子，名叫王献之。他十分聪慧，从小跟随父亲学习书法、绘画，技艺日益精熟。他在还是少年的时候就很有名气了。

据说有一次，父亲的学生们在玩樗蒲游戏。他站在旁边观看，发现有个人要输了，便说："南边的风力不强。"那个人听王献之说自己要输了，心里很不高兴，就白了他一眼，讥笑他说："这个小孩就像从管子里看豹，只看见豹子身上的

一小块斑点，却看不到整只豹子。"王献之听了，

觉得受到轻视，就很生气地说："你们不要小看

人！远的，我惭愧不如荀奉倩；近的，我惭愧不如

刘真长。"他意思是自己的才学优于一般人，只自

愧不如荀奉倩、刘真长这两个人。他一说完，就

转身离开了。

后来，王献之发奋努力，经过长期的勤学苦

练，终于成了著名书法家，与他的父亲王羲之

名声一样大，被后世并称为"二王"。

In the Jin Dynasty, the famous calligrapher Wang Xizhi had a son named Wang Xianzhi, who was very famous since he was a teenager. He learned handwriting and painting from his father, and his skills got increasingly refined.

It is said that once watching his father's students playing Chupu, he found that someone was going to lose, so he said,

"The south wind is not strong." The man felt very unpleasant after hearing Wang Xianzhi's prediction that he was going to lose，so he looked hard at him and mocked him by saying "The child just looks at a leopard through a pipe. He could only see the spot rather than the whole leopard". Wang Xianzhi felt despised and annoyed，so he said，"Don't look down on me. Among ancestors，I am just inferior to Xun Fengqian. Among contemporaries，I am just not as excellent as Liu Zhenchang." He meant that he just felt humble to these two scholars. After saying this，he stopped talking with them and left.

From then on，Wang Xianzhi tried hard to practice calligraphy and finally became an outstanding calligrapher as famous as his father. And the father and son were called as "two Wangs".

生难字/词注解 │ Notes

樗蒲： 古代的一种游戏，类似掷骰子游戏。

Chupu： A kind of game played in ancient times similar to throwing dices.

荀奉倩： 即荀粲，颍川颍阴人，三国时曹魏名士。为人清高，很有才学，不与俗人交往。

Xun Fengqian： Also named Xun Can, born in Yinchuan, a famous scholar in the State of Wei during the Three Kingdoms period. He is learned and aloof from mundane affairs and people.

刘真长： 即刘惔，东晋官员，为人清高，和荀奉倩是同一类人物。

Liu Zhenchang: Also named Liu Tan, an official in the Eastern Jin Dynasty. He also holds himself aloof just like Xun Fengqian.

故事寓意 | The moral of the story

"管中窥豹"是指从竹管的小孔里看豹，只看到豹子身上的一块斑纹。用来比喻只看到事物的一部分，没有看到事物的全部，因而见识偏颇。

"To see only one spot of leopard through a pipe" means that if you watch the leopard through the hole of a bamboo pipe, you could just see one spot on the leopard's body. It is often used to describe that people would be biased if they only see a part of something instead of the whole of it.

139

井底之蛙

The Frog at the Bottom of a Well

yì zhī qīng wā　　zhù zài yì kǒu xiá xiǎo de shuǐ jǐng lǐ　　tā duì zì jǐ
一只青蛙，住在一口狭小的水井里，它对自己

shēng huó de dì fang shí fēn mǎn yì
生活的地方十分满意。

yì tiān　　qīng wā zài jǐng biān pèng dào yì zhī cóng dōng hǎi lái de dà hǎi
一天，青蛙在井边碰到一只从东海来的大海

guī　　biàn xiàng dà hǎi guī chuī shī jǐng dǐ duō me guǎng kuò yǔ yǒu qù　　tā
龟。便向大海龟吹嘘井底多么广阔与有趣，它

shuō　　nǐ qiáo wǒ zhù zài zhèr　　duō me kuài huó ya　　gāo xìng shí　　jiù zài
说："你瞧我住在这儿多么快活呀！高兴时，就在

jǐng lǐ tiào lái tiào qù　　lèi le kě yǐ zài jǐng bì de féng xì lǐ xiū xi　　wǒ
井里跳来跳去，累了可以在井壁的缝隙里休息，我

shì jǐng lǐ de zhǔ rén　　duō me zì yóu zì zài ya　　shuō zhe　　qīng wā yāo qǐng
是井里的主人，多么自由自在呀。"说着，青蛙邀请

海龟到井里去游玩，海龟打算到井里去看看，可是，刚要进去时，一只腿就被井边的石块绊住了。

它进退不得，只好慢慢地退回到井台上。

过了一会儿，海龟问青蛙："你听说过大海吗？"青蛙摇摇头说："没有"。接着，海龟告诉青蛙大海如何宽广："大海里的水无边无际，非常辽阔。传说四千多年以前，大禹做国君的时候，十年当中有九年会发生大洪水，但是海水没有因此加深；三千多年以前，商汤做国君的年代，八年中有七年发生旱灾，但是海水并没有减少。大海是这样广大，不管是时间还是旱涝，都不能使它的水量发生明显的变化。青蛙兄弟，我就生活在大海中。你看，比起你这口枯井，哪个更广阔，哪个乐趣更大呢？"

青蛙这才知道，井外还有这么广大的天地，它

yòu jīng qí yòu cán kuì　gǎn dào zì jǐ de jiàn shi tài miǎo xiǎo le
又惊奇又惭愧，感到自己的见识太渺小了。

There was a frog living at the bottom of a small well. It was very satisfied with its place.

One day，the frog met a turtle from the East Sea at the edge of the well，so he boasted to the turtle about its wide and interesting well. "Look. How happy I am in this place! When I feel happy，I could jump here and there in the well. When I'm tired，I could rest in the gap of holes on the broken wall of the well. I am the Lord of this well." Then the frog invited the turtle to have a look and play in the well. Before the turtle could get in the well，one of its legs got stuck in the stones. It hesitated and retreated.

After a while，the turtle asked the frog，"Have you heard of the sea?" The frog shook its head and said "Never". Then the turtle told the frog about the sea，"The sea is boundlessly wide. As legend has it，about four thousand years ago，in the time of Emperor Yu，there were floods for nine years out of ten，but the water in the sea did not increase. About three thousand years ago，in the time of King Tang of the Shang Dynasty，there were droughts for seven years out of eight，but the water in the sea did not decrease. The sea does not change with the passage of time and its level does not rise or fall according to the amount of rainfall. Buddy，I live in the sea. The sea and your well，which is wider and more interesting?"

After listening to these words, the frog of the shallow well was shocked into realization of his own insignificance and felt ashamed for his tininess.

生难字/词注解 | Note

缝隙：指接合处或裂开的空处。
Gap：Space between two things or a hole in the middle of something solid.

故事寓意 | The moral of the story

"井底之蛙"常常用来讽刺那些见识短浅而又唯我独尊的人。这个故事告诉我们：要清醒地自我定位，不断地去学习，开阔眼界，增长见识。

"The frog at the bottom of a well" is often used to satirize those narrow-minded and arrogant people. This story tells us that we should know ourselves and continue to acquire knowledge and broaden our horizon.

假秀才招打

The Fake Scholar Asking for Trouble

gǔ shí hou　yǒu yí dà hù rén jiā de ér zi shēng xìng lǎn duò　hào
古时候，有一大户人家的儿子 生 性懒惰、好

wán lè　cóng xiǎo jiù bù xǐ huān dú shū　zhè ge rén zhǎng dà hòu xíng wéi
玩乐，从小就不喜欢读书。这个人长大后行为

jǔ zhǐ shí fēn cū bǐ　yú chǔn　shí zài ràng rén yàn wù　bù jǐn rú cǐ
举止十分粗鄙、愚蠢，实在让人厌恶。不仅如此，

tā hái hěn xǐ huān chuī xū　chángcháng jiǎ zhuāng zì jǐ wú suǒ bù zhī
他还很喜欢吹嘘，常常假装自己无所不知。

　　yí cì　tā yào dào guān fǔ qù gào zhuàng　wèi le qǔ dé xiàn guān
一次，他要到官府去告状。为了取得县官

de xìn rèn　tā bǎ zì jǐ dǎ bàn chéng yí gè shū shēng de mú yàng　piàn xiàn
的信任，他把自己打扮成一个书生的模样，骗县

guān shuō tā shì xiù cai　xiàn guān hěn jīng yà　yǎn qián de zhè ge rén xíng wéi
官说他是秀才。县官很惊讶，眼前的这个人行为

jǔ zhǐ dōu hěn cū lǔ　nǎ lǐ xiàng shì xiù cai a　xiàn guān hěn huái yí
举止都很粗鲁，哪里像是秀才啊！县官很怀疑，

于是就设计试探。县官问他:"刚才你说你是秀才,那你先说说'桓公杀子纠'这一章讲述的是什么内容呢?"其实这个人并没有读过书,他不知道县官是在考他,"桓公杀子纠"是《论语》里的句子。这个无知的人,听到县官这样说,心里害怕极了,他以为县官是在审问他是否杀了人。于是,他急忙辩解道:"县官老爷,我冤枉啊,我确实不知道这个案子的实情啊,还请您明察,这确实不关小人的事啊!"县官听了,既生气又觉得好笑,心想:"你竟敢骗我,看我怎么收拾你!"县官下令,将这人捆绑起来,用木棍狠狠地打了他二十下,打得他皮肉都裂开了,痛得他哇哇直叫。

这人挨了打之后,就被县官赶回家了。在路上,他对仆人说:"这位县官太不讲理了,硬说我父亲打死了翁小九。他不仅冤枉了父亲,还打了我二十大板。"仆人问清楚事情的缘由之后说：

"'桓公杀子纠'是书上的一句话呀，你如果不知

道，可以简单应付一下，就说你不曾阅读过这本书

就可以了。"这人使劲摇摇头说："你不要再害我

了，我连说不知道还被他打了二十大板，如果说知

道一点点，那他岂不是要抓我去偿命吗？"仆人

听了，对他的无知感到可笑。

In ancient times, there was a boy born in a big family who was lazy and pleasure-seeking. He didn't like reading since his childhood. When he grew up, his behavior was vulgar, foolish, and annoying. And he also enjoyed boasting about himself and always pretended that he knew everything.

Once, he went to the local authorities to sue. In order to make the magistrate trust him, he dressed up like an intellectual and claimed to be a scholar. The magistrate was so surprised that how this rude man could be a scholar. Doubting whether this man was a scholar, he planned to test him. The magistrate asked,

"Since you said you're a scholar, can you tell me about the content of 'Duke Huan killed Zijiu'?" Actually, the man had never read any books, and didn't know the magistrate was testing him. "Duke Huan killed Zijiu" was a sentence from *The Analects*. After hearing the magistrate's question, the ignorant man was extremely terrified because he thought the magistrate was questioning him if he had killed someone. In consequence, he defended hastily, "Magistrate, I'm innocent and I really don't know the case. I beg you to investigate this case thoroughly, which is really none of my business." After that, the magistrate felt both angry and ridiculous, he wondered, "How dare a fake scholar come to cheat me. You shall get punished." Then, the magistrate ordered the guards to tie the young man up and beat him 20 times with a big board. The man kept yelling in pain and his flesh was torn out.

The man was driven back home after being beaten. On the way, he said to his servant, "The magistrate unreasonably insisted that my father had killed Weng Xiaojiu. Not only did he wrong my father, but hit me 20 times with the board." After asking the matter in detail, the servant said, "'Duke Huan killed Zijiu' is a sentence in a book. If you don't know about it, you can just try to muddle through and state you have never read it." The man shook his head emphatically and said, "Don't get me into trouble. I have been hit 20 times just because I said I didn't know. If I say that I know something about it, wouldn't he take my life?" After hearing this, the servant felt ridiculous about his ignorance.

生难字/词注解 | Note

秀才：古代中国选拔官吏的科目；亦用以称书生、读书人的一种称呼。

Xiucai: A kind of imperial examination system in ancient China. And also refers to scholars.

故事寓意 | The moral of the story

这个故事告诉我们：为人处世要诚实，不说谎，不作假。如果像"假秀才"那样假装学识渊博，到处去说谎、欺骗别人，一旦被识破，就会给自己带来麻烦。

This story tells us that we should be honest and never cheat or tell lies. If one pretends to be erudite and cheats others just like the "fake scholar", it would cause himself trouble when it is uncovered.

刻舟求剑

Marking on the Boat Side for a Sunk Sword

zhàn guó shí qī　　yǒu yí gè chǔ guó rén chū mén yuǎn xíng　　tā zài zuò
战国时期，有一个楚国人出门远行。他在坐

chuán dù jiāng de shí hou　　yí bù xiǎo xīn suí shēn pèi dài de bǎo jiàn diào dào
船渡江的时候，一不小心，随身佩带的宝剑掉到

le jiāng shuǐ zhōng　　zuò zài tóng yì sōu chuán shang de rén dōu hěn zháo jí
了江水中。坐在同一艘船上的人都很着急，

dà jiào qǐ lái　　jiàn diào jìn shuǐ lǐ le　　kě shì zhè ge chǔ guó rén què bù
大叫起来："剑掉进水里了。"可是这个楚国人却不

huāng bù máng de yòng yì bǎ xiǎo dāo　　zài chuán xián biān shang kè le yí gè
慌不忙地用一把小刀，在船舷边上刻了一个

jì hao　　rán hòu　　huí tóu duì dà jiā shuō　　zhè shì wǒ de jiàn diào xià qù
记号。然后，回头对大家说："这是我的剑掉下去

de dì fang　　yǒu rén cuī cù tā shuō　　kuài xià shuǐ qù zhǎo jiàn ya　　chǔ
的地方。"有人催促他说："快下水去找剑呀！"楚

guó rén shuō　　huāng shén me　　wǒ yǒu jì hao ne　　chuán jì xù qián xíng
国人说："慌什么，我有记号呢。"船继续前行，

又有人催他说："再不下去找剑，这船越走越远，当心找不回来了。"楚国人依旧自信地说："不用急，不用急，记号刻在那儿呢。"大家对这个楚国人的行为很困惑，但都说服不了他及时去找剑。

船一路行驶，终于靠岸了。这个楚国人才顺着他刻有记号的地方下水去找剑。找了很长时间，都没有看见宝剑，他觉得很奇怪，说："我的宝剑在这里掉下去的，我还在这里刻了记号呢，怎么会找不到呢？"大家都讥笑他，说："你的剑掉下去，沉到了水底，而船却开走了。这个时候你怎么能找得到你的剑呢？"结果他在船靠岸的地方找寻了很久，却白费了工夫，他什么都没有找到。

During the Warring States period, a man from the State of Chu went on a long journey with his sword. When he was on a boat, he dropped his sword into the water accidentally. Other people in the same boat felt pity for him, but he was quite confident. Calmly he took out a knife, carved a mark on the the side of the boat, and said, "This is where my sword fell into the water." Someone urged him, "Jump into the water to find your sword!" The man said calmly, "Don't panic. I have made the sign." The boat went on, and some of them urged him again, "The boat is going farther. If you don't go down to find your sword, you may never find it." The man still said confidently, "Don't worry, don't worry. The mark is still here." Everyone was confused by the man's behavior, but nobody could persuade him to find the sword.

The boat moved forward all the way and finally reached the other bank. The man from the State of Chu jumped into the water from the very place where he had made the mark. After a long period of time, he still could not find the sword. He felt puzzled and said, "My sword just dropped from this point and I have marked a sign here. Why can't I find it?" People laughed at him and said, "The boat has left that point, and your sword has sunk into the bottom of the water. How can you find your sword?" The person spent much time looking for his sword near the shore where the boat pulled in, but found nothing at all.

故事寓意 | The moral of the story

"刻舟求剑"用来讽刺做事迂腐、不知道事物会变化的人。这个故事告诉我们：世界上万事万物总是在不断地发展变化，我们不能用静止的眼光去看待，而应该考虑并适应这种变化，灵活地去想问题、做事情。

"Marking on a boat side for a sunk sword" is used to satirize people who are pedantic and disregard the changing circumstances. The story tells us that everything in the world is constantly changing and we shouldn't look at it in a static way. We should make changes according to specific conditions, and consider and settle things flexibly.

滥竽充数

Be There Just to Make Up the Number

zhàn guó shí hou   qí guó de guó jūn qí xuān wáng fēi cháng xǐ huān tīng
战国时候，齐国的国君齐宣王非常喜欢听

chuī yú   qí xuān wáng xǐ hào rè nao   ài bǎi pái chǎng   měi cì tīng chuī yú
吹竽。齐宣王喜好热闹，爱摆排场，每次听吹竽

de shí hou   zǒng shì jiào sān bǎi duō rén tóng shí chuī gěi tā tīng   yǒu yí ge
的时候，总是叫三百多人同时吹给他听。有一个

nán guō xiān sheng   tā běn lái bú huì chuī yú   dàn tā zài qí xuān wáng miàn
南郭先生，他本来不会吹竽，但他在齐宣王面

qián chuī xū zì jǐ shì ge yǒu míng de yuè shī   qí xuān wáng xìn yǐ wéi
前吹嘘自己是个有名的乐师。齐宣王信以为

zhēn   jiù jiào tā hé nà sān bǎi duō rén yí kuàir   yǎn zòu   nán guō xiān sheng
真，就叫他和那三百多人一块儿演奏。南郭先生

shí fēn dé yì   měi cì dào yǎn zòu de shí hou   tā jiù jiǎ zhuāng hé qí tā
十分得意，每次到演奏的时候，他就假装和其他

rén yí yàng yáo tóu huàng nǎo   zhuāng zuò hěn tóu rù hěn dòng qíng de mú yàng
人一样摇头晃脑，装作很投入很动情的模样。

tā jiù zhè yàng méng hùn zhe guò guān   bù láo ér huò de ná zhe yōu hòu de xīn
他就这样蒙混着过关，不劳而获地拿着优厚的薪

shuǐ hé shǎng cì
水 和 赏 赐 。

hòu lái qí xuān wáng sǐ le tā de ér zi qí mǐn wáng jì chéng le
后来，齐宣王死了，他的儿子齐湣王继承了

wáng wèi qí mǐn wáng yě xǐ huān tīng chuī yú kě shì tā xǐ huān dān dú
王位。齐湣王也喜欢听吹竽，可是他喜欢单独

yí gè rén chuī yú gěi tā tīng yuè shī men zhī dào hòu gèng jiā nǔ lì de
一个人吹竽给他听。乐师们知道后，更加努力地

liàn xí zhǐ yǒu nà ge sā huǎng de nán guō xiān sheng hěn zháo jí tā
练习。只有那个撒谎的南郭先生很着急。他

xiǎng lái xiǎng qù jué de zhè cì zài yě méng hùn bú guò qù le zhǐ hǎo tōu
想来想去，觉得这次再也蒙混不过去了，只好偷

tōu de liū zǒu le
偷地溜走了。

During the Warring States period, King Xuan of the State of Qi was very fond of listening to Yu, a kind of flute. He also enjoyed jollification and often got over 300 Yu players to perform together.

A man named Nanguo didn't know how to play the instrument, but he bragged that he was a famous musician in front of the king. The king believed him and ordered him to play with other three hundred players. Mr. Nanguo was very complacent and pretended to play devotedly, shaking his head and body. As a result, he enjoyed a fat income and reward just as other musicians did.

When King Xuan died, his son Min became the new ruler who also liked the music played on Yu. However, he preferred solos so that all the musicians practiced even harder. Nanguo was anxious and he knew he couldn't bluff it out anymore. Therefore, Nanguo had to sneak out of the palace.

生难字/词注解 | Note

竽：古代簧管乐器，形似笙而较大，有三十六簧管。 战国至汉代曾广泛流传。
Yu：A kind of ancient musical instrument made by reed pipes.

故事寓意 | The moral of the story

"滥竽充数"用来比喻没有真才实学却要冒充很内行。这个故事告诉我们：想要获得成功,最重要的是勤奋学习,坚持不懈地努力,只有拥有过硬的本领,我们才能经受住一切考验。

"Be there just to make up the number" is used to mock people who pretend to be experts without solid learning. The story tells us that in order to succeed, we should be industrious and keep making constant efforts. Only with a solid foundation, can we become capable and stand any test.

买椟还珠

Getting the Casket and Returning the Pearl

chūn qiū shí qī　　yǒu yí gè chǔ guó rén　tā yǒu yì　kē piào liang de
春 秋 时 期 ，有 一 个 楚 国 人 ，他 有 一 颗 漂 亮 的

zhēn zhū　dǎ suàn mài chū qù　　wèi le néng gòu mài gè hǎo de jià qián　　tā
珍 珠 ，打 算 卖 出 去 。为 了 能 够 卖 个 好 的 价 钱 ，他

jué de yīng gāi bǎ zhēn zhū jīng xīn bāo zhuāng yí xià　　yú shì　　tā zhǎo lái
觉 得 应 该 把 珍 珠 精 心 包 装 一 下 。于 是 ，他 找 来

míng guì de mù cái　　yòu qǐng lái shǒu yì gāo chāo de jiàng rén　wèi zhēn zhū zuò
名 贵 的 木 材 ，又 请 来 手 艺 高 超 的 匠 人 ，为 珍 珠 做

le yí gè hé zi　　zài hé zi de wài céng hái tè yì diāo kè le xǔ duō hǎo
了 一 个 盒 子 ，在 盒 子 的 外 层 还 特 意 雕 刻 了 许 多 好

kàn de huā wén　　hé　zi kàn shàng qù xiàng shì yí jiàn jīng zhì měi guān de gōng
看 的 花 纹 。盒 子 看 上 去 像 是 一 件 精 致 美 观 的 工

yì pǐn　　　chǔ guó rén duì zhè ge hé　zi shí fēn mǎn yì　　tā jiāng zhēn zhū xiǎo
艺 品 。楚 国 人 对 这 个 盒 子 十 分 满 意 ，他 将 珍 珠 小

心翼翼地放进盒子里,拿到市场上去卖。

刚到市场上,就有很多人围上来观看这个精美的盒子。其中,有一个郑国人,将盒子看了又看,非常喜爱。他愿意付出高昂的价钱买这个盒子。郑国人付过钱后,便拿着盒子走了。过了一会儿,他又回来了。只见他将盒子打开,取出里面的珍珠,交给那个楚国人,说:"你将一颗珍珠放在盒子里了,我特意回来还你珠子的。"

楚国人拿着被退回来的珍珠,十分尴尬地站在那里。他原本以为别人会欣赏他的珍珠,可是没想到别人更加喜欢精美的盒子,这真是令他哭笑不得呀。

During the Spring and Autumn period, a man in the State of Chu had a beautiful pearl. In order to sell it at a good price, he decided to pack it in a nice way. So he found a piece of luxury wood, and asked a skillful craftsman to make a casket for the pearl. The casket was carved with many beautiful floral patterns, looking like a delicate work of art. The man was very satisfied with the box, and he put the pearl into it with great care and went to the market.

Just after he arrived at the market, a lot of people came around to watch this beautiful box. Among them, there was a man from the State of Zheng who was very fond of the box and would like to pay a high price for it. The man from the State of Zheng paid and left with the box. After a while, he returned. He opened the box, took the pearl out and gave it back to the man from the State of Chu and said, "There is a pearl in the box and I am back to return it." Taking the pearl, the man from the State of Chu stood there awkwardly.

He had thought that others would appreciate his pearl, but it turned out that others liked the beautiful casket more. It was really funny and annoying.

生难字/词注解 | Note

椟：木柜，匣子，特指宝盒。

Casket：A wooden and often ornate box for holding jewels or other valuables.

故事寓意 | The moral of the story

"买椟还珠"用来比喻没有眼光，取舍不当。这个故事告诉我们：在做事情的时候要认清事情的本相，不要轻重不分，本末倒置。

"Getting the casket and returning the pearl" is used to describe people who have no vision and don't know how to make the right choice. The story tells us that we should find out the truth and not put the incidental before the fundamental.

杞人忧天

The Man of Qi Worries in Case the Sky Should Fall

春秋时期，杞国有一个胆子很小的人，总是喜欢胡思乱想。一天，他竟然想到天会塌下来，地会陷下去，自己去哪里安身？从此，他几乎每天为这个问题烦恼，忧愁得吃不下饭，也睡不着觉。

朋友看见他这样愁苦，就去开导他，说："天不过是由大气聚集而成的，你天天在这中间呼吸、活动，为什么要担心它会塌下来呢？"那个杞国人听了，又问："如果天是一些积聚的气体，那么天

shàng de tài yáng yuè liang xīng xing huì bu huì diào xià lái ne péng you
上 的 太 阳 、月 亮 、星 星 ,会 不 会 掉 下 来 呢 ?"朋 友

shuō tài yáng yuè liang xīng xing yě dōu shì yóu qì tǐ zǔ chéng de zhǐ
说 :"太 阳 、月 亮 、星 星 也 都 是 由 气 体 组 成 的 ,只

bú guò néng fā guāng bà le kě shì qǐ guó rén de yōu lù hái méi yǒu wán
不 过 能 发 光 罢 了 。"可 是 杞 国 人 的 忧 虑 还 没 有 完 ,

tā jiē zhe wèn nà yào shì dì xiàn xià qù le ne yòu gāi zěn me bàn
他 接 着 问 :"那 要 是 地 陷 下 去 了 呢 ? 又 该 怎 么 办 ?"

tā de péng you gào su tā dì shì yóu gè zhǒng ní tǔ zǔ chéng de nǐ
他 的 朋 友 告 诉 他 :"地 是 由 各 种 泥 土 组 成 的 ,你

tiān tiān dōu zài shàng miàn zǒu lù huó dòng nǎ huì xiàn xià qù ne nǐ gēn
天 天 都 在 上 面 走 路 活 动 ,哪 会 陷 下 去 呢 ? 你 根

běn bú yòng dān xīn a tīng le péng you de quàn dǎu hòu zhè ge qǐ guó rén
本 不 用 担 心 啊 !"听 了 朋 友 的 劝 导 后 ,这 个 杞 国 人

zhōng yú fàng xià xīn le
终 于 放 下 心 了 。

During the Spring and Autumn period, in the State of Qi there was a man who was very cowardly and always let his imagination run away with him. One day he even worried that the sky would fall on his head and the ground would sink. He was so worried that he could neither eat nor sleep.

Seeing him so distressed, one of his friends persuaded him, "The sky is formed by the air and you breathe and move in it every day. Why do you bother to worry about the fall of it?" The man asked after hearing this，"If the sky is made up of gases，would the Sun，the Moon and the stars fall down?" His friend replied，"The Sun，the Moon and the stars are also made of gases，and the only difference between them and the sky is that they could shine." But the man still felt anxious and asked，"What if the ground sinks? What should we do?" His friend told him，"The ground is made of all kinds of earth which you walk on every day. Has it ever sunk? You really don't need to worry about that." After his friend's persuasion，the man finally felt relieved.

故事寓意 | The moral of the story

"杞人忧天"常用来比喻那些没有必要的担心和忧虑。这个故事告诉我们：不要为一些不切实际的事情而自寻烦恼，我们要心境开阔，做一个豁达、乐观的人。

"The man of Qi worries in case the sky should fall" satirizes those who worry unnecessarily. The story tells us that we shouldn't ask for trouble ourselves with unrealistic things. Instead，we should be open-minded and optimistic.

神鸟与猫头鹰

The Mythical Bird and the Owl

庄子是一个性情洒脱、淡泊名利的哲学家。

他有一个好朋友，名叫惠施，被封为魏国的宰

相。庄子听说后，十分高兴，打算去拜访他。

可是奸诈小人知道庄子要去拜访惠施后，就在惠

施面前说庄子坏话。惠施听信小人的谗言，下

令抓捕庄子。

然而，庄子却冒着被抓捕的危险，直接去见

惠施，他说："我讲个故事给你听吧。在南方，传

shuō yǒu yì zhǒng shén niǎo yǔ fèng huáng yí yàng gāo guì míng jiào yuān chú
说有一种神鸟，与凤凰一样高贵，名叫鹓鶵。

tā cóng nán hǎi chū fā fēi dào běi hǎi zài zhè màn cháng de lù tú zhōng
它从南海出发，飞到北海，在这漫长的路途中，

rú guǒ méi yǒu kàn jiàn gāo gāo de wú tóng shù jué duì bú huì tíng xià lái xiū
如果没有看见高高的梧桐树，绝对不会停下来休

xi rú guǒ bú shì qīng qīng de cuì zhú yǔ míng guì de guǒ shí jué duì bú huì
息；如果不是青青的翠竹与名贵的果实，绝对不会

shí yòng méi yǒu yù dào gān tián de quán shuǐ jué duì bú huì yǐn yòng zhè
食用；没有遇到甘甜的泉水，绝对不会饮用。这

zhī dà niǎo yí lù fēi xiáng zài tiān kōng kàn jiàn dì miàn shang yǒu zhī māo tóu
只大鸟一路飞翔，在天空看见地面上有只猫头

yīng zhèng zài zhuó shí yì zhī fǔ làn de sǐ lǎo shǔ māo tóu yīng fēi cháng
鹰，正在啄食一只腐烂的死老鼠。猫头鹰非常

jī è kàn jiàn zài tóu dǐng fēi xiáng de dà niǎo hòu yǐ wéi shì lái qiǎng duó
饥饿，看见在头顶飞翔的大鸟后，以为是来抢夺

tā de sǐ lǎo shǔ de tā fēi cháng fèn nù duì zhe dà niǎo fā chū kǒng hè
它的死老鼠的，它非常愤怒，对着大鸟发出恐吓

de hǎn jiào
的喊叫。"

zhuāng zǐ jiǎng wán gù shi hòu wèn huì shī nín huò fēng le wèi guó
庄子讲完故事后，问惠施："您获封了魏国

de xiàng wèi hài pà wǒ huì duó qǔ shì bu shì yě yào duì wǒ kǒng hè yì fān
的相位，害怕我会夺取，是不是也要对我恐吓一番

ne shuō wán zhuāng zǐ dà shēng de xiào qǐ lái zǒu chū mén qù le
呢？"说完，庄子大声地笑起来，走出门去了。

Zhuangzi was a free and easygoing philosopher who was indifferent to fame and wealth. He had a good friend named Hui Shi who was appointed as the Prime Minister in the State of Wei. After hearing this news, Zhuangzi was very glad and decided to pay a visit to him. But when some treacherous villains knew this, they went to Hui Shi and said something bad about Zhuangzi. Hui Shi believed their aspersion and gave order to arrest Zhuangzi.

Facing the danger of being caught, Zhuangzi went directly to Hui Shi and said, "Let me tell you a story. In the south, legend has it that once there was a kind of fairy bird called Yuanchu who was as noble as phoenix. It moved from the South Sea to the North Sea, and during its long journey, it would not stop to rest without finding a tall phoenix tree, to eat without finding great bamboo and precious fruit, or to drink without finding sweet spring water. During its flight, it saw an owl on the ground, pecking at a rotting dead mouse. The owl was very hungry, and when it saw the bird over its head, it thought the bird was about to rob the dead mouse. It got very furious and shouted to scare the bird away."

After telling the story, Zhuangzi asked Hui Shi, "You've got the position of Prime Minister in the State of Wei. Are you going to threaten me because you think I am going to grab it from you?" Then, Zhuangzi laughed out loudly and walked out of the room.

故事寓意 | The moral of the story

庄子以高贵的鹓鶵自喻，表明自己品行高洁，不屑与小人同流合污。这个故事告诉我们：奸诈小人往往用阴暗心理来揣测别人。我们只要心地坦荡，做事光明磊落，就不必害怕小人的流言中伤。

Zhuangzi compared himself to the bird called Yuanchu to illustrate his noble nature and his unwillingness to wallow in the mire with villains. The story tells us that treacherous people always speculate on others from a dark perspective. As long as we are broad-minded and behave in a fair and square manner, we don't need to be afraid of being maligned by villains' gossip.

乌鸦兄弟

The Crow Brothers

wū yā xiōng dì liǎ yì qǐ zhù zài tóng yí gè wō cháo lǐ　　yǒu yì
乌鸦兄弟俩一起住在同一个窝巢里。有一

tiān wō cháo pò le yí gè dòng dà wū yā xiǎng　　lǎo èr huì qù xiū
天,窝巢破了一个洞,大乌鸦想:"老二会去修

de xiǎo wū yā xiǎng　　lǎo dà huì qù xiū de　　jié guǒ shéi yě méi yǒu
的。"小乌鸦想:"老大会去修的。"结果谁也没有

qù xiū
去修。

shí jiān yì tiān yì tiān guò qù　　hòu lái dòng yuè lái yuè dà le　　dà wū
时间一天一天过去,后来洞越来越大了。大乌

yā xiǎng　　zhè yí xià lǎo èr yí dìng huì qù xiū le　　nán dào wō cháo zhè
鸦想:"这一下老二一定会去修了,难道窝巢这

yàng pò le　　tā hái néng zhù de xià qù ma　　xiǎo wū yā xiǎng　　zhè yí
样破了,它还能住得下去吗?"小乌鸦想:"这一

下老大一定会去修了，难道窝巢这样破了，它还能住下去吗？"结果又是谁也没有去修。

寒冷的冬天到了，西北风呼呼地刮着。下大雪了，乌鸦兄弟俩都蜷缩在破烂的窝巢里，被冻得直打哆嗦。它们禁不住叫着："好冷啊！好冷啊！"大乌鸦想："这样冷的天气，老二一定经受不住了，它肯定会去修了。"小乌鸦想："这样冷的天气，老大还经受得住吗？它肯定会去修了。"可是谁也没有动手去修补一下破败的窝，只是把身子蜷缩得更紧些。

风越刮越厉害，雪越下越大。结果，窝巢被风吹到地上，两只乌鸦被冻僵了。

The crow brothers lived together in the same nest. One day, a hole appeared in the nest, but the elder crow thought, "My younger brother will go to repair it." The younger crow thought, "My elder brother will go to repair it." Eventually no one did anything.

Days passed and later the hole became bigger and bigger, but the older brother still thought, "Well, now my little brother would definitely repair it. How could he live in such a shabby nest?" The younger crow also thought, "My elder brother must go to repair it this time. How could he keep living in the nest with such a big hole?" But it turned out that nobody repaired it.

When the cold winter came, the wind whistled and it snowed heavily. The crow brothers both huddled in their tattered nest and shivered out of coldness. They couldn't help crying, "How cold! How cold!" The older crow thought, "On such a cold day, my brother could not bear it anymore, and he must go to mend the nest." The younger crow thought, "Could my brother stand such a cold day? He sure would go fix the nest." But nobody did anything, and they just curled their bodies closer.

The wind blew harder and harder, and the snow became heavier and heavier. Finally the nest was blown down to the ground, and the crow brothers were frozen stiff.

生难字/词注解 | Notes

蜷缩：身躯蜷曲紧缩。
Cuddle：Curl the body together.

窝巢：禽兽、昆虫的居住地。
Nest：A place where birds, beasts, and insects live.

故事寓意 | The moral of the story

　　这个故事比喻做事相互推脱，自己不主动解决问题，反而依赖别人去解决问题，结果会自食其果，不得善终。这个故事告诉我们：要有责任感，勇于承担，去做好本分的事情。

This story satirizes that people who evade responsibility and don't take the initiative to solve problems would suffer from the consequences. We should be brave to face our responsibility and fulfill our duty.

心不在马

Focusing Not on the Horses

zhàn guó shí qī　zhào xiāng wáng xiàng wáng zǐ qī xué xí jià yù mǎ
战国时期，赵襄王向王子期学习驾驭马

chē　gāng gāng xué xí méi yǒu duō cháng shí jiān　tā jiù yào yǔ wáng zǐ qī
车。刚刚学习没有多长时间，他就要与王子期

bǐ sài　kàn shéi de mǎ chē pǎo de kuài　kě shì　tā yì lián huàn le sān cì
比赛，看谁的马车跑得快。可是，他一连换了三次

mǎ　jìn xíng le sān chǎng bǐ sài　měi cì dōu yuǎn yuǎn de là zài wáng zǐ qī
马，进行了三场比赛，每次都远远地落在王子期

de hòu miàn
的后面。

zhào xiāng wáng hěn bù gāo xìng　bǎ wáng zǐ qī jiào dào shēn biān　zhǐ
赵襄王很不高兴，把王子期叫到身边，指

zé tā shuō　nǐ jì rán jiāo wǒ jià chē　wèi shén me bù jiāng zhēn běn lǐng wán
责他说："你既然教我驾车，为什么不将真本领完

quán jiāo gěi wǒ ne　nǐ nán dào hái xiǎng yǒu suǒ bǎo liú ma　wáng zǐ qī
全教给我呢？你难道还想有所保留吗？"王子期

回答说："驾车的方法、技巧，我已经全部教给大王了。只是您在运用的时候忘记了要领。一般说来，驾车时最重要的是使马在车辕里松紧适度，自在舒适。而驾车人的注意力则要集中在马的身上。要沉住气，让人与马的动作相互协调，这样才可以使车跑得快，跑得远。可是刚才您在与我比赛的时候，只要稍有落后，您就着急，使劲鞭打着马，拼命要超过我。而一旦跑到了我的前面，又时常回头观望，害怕我再赶上您。总之，不论领先还是落后，您心情都十分紧张，您的注意力几乎全部集中在比赛的输赢上了，却不顾马的死活，这怎么可能驾好马车呢？这就是您失败的根本原因啊。"

During the Warring States period, King Xiang of the State of Zhao learned how to ride carriage from Wang Ziqi. Quite soon, he wanted to compete with Wang Ziqi. He changed his horses and competed for three times, but every time he fell far behind.

The king was very unpleasant, and he summoned Wang Ziqi and scolded him, "Why don't you teach me all your skills? Do you still want to keep something to yourself?" Wang Ziqi replied, "I have taught you all the methods and skills of driving, but you forgot them when you were practicing. Generally speaking, the most important thing is to make the horses feel comfortable in their shafts. The rider should focus on the horses. Keep calm and coordinate the actions of the horses and yourself. Only in this way could horses run faster and farther. While just now, you whipped the horses violently when you fell behind, and you looked back when you surpassed me, being afraid of me catching up with you. All in all, you felt nervous when you were either in front of or behind me. You focused on the winning rather than the situation of the horses. How could you possibly ride fast? This is the real reason that you failed."

故事寓意 | The moral of the story

这个故事告诉我们：无论做什么事，都要专心致志，更多地关注过程，而不是在乎结果。如果过多计较胜负输赢，我们就会患得患失，为名利所累，结果往往会事与愿违，把事情弄糟。

This story tells us that no matter what we do, we should focus on and pay attention to the process instead of the result. If we care too much about winning or losing, we will worry about gain and loss and get encumbered with fame and fortune. Things would be contrary to what we expect and become worse instead.

新媳妇

The Newly-wed Wife

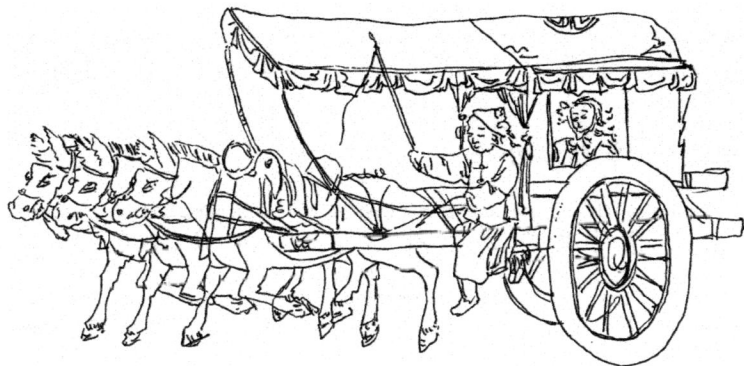

wèi guó yǒu hù rén jiā qǔ xí fu　　jiā lǐ zhǐ yǒu yì pǐ mǎ　　wèi le
卫国有户人家娶媳妇，家里只有一匹马。为了

shùn lì jǔ xíng hūn lǐ　　tā men zhǐ hǎo xiàng lín jū jiè lái liǎng pǐ mǎ　　yí
顺利举行婚礼，他们只好向邻居借来两匹马，一

gòng sān pǐ mǎ　　chéng qīn nà rì　　fū jiā yòng sān pǐ mǎ lā zhe chē　　rè
共三匹马。成亲那日，夫家用三匹马拉着车，热

rè nào nào de qù yíng jiē xīn niáng zi　　yíng qīn de rén jiāng xīn niáng zi fú
热闹闹地去迎接新娘子。迎亲的人将新娘子扶

shàng le mǎ chē　　jiù chū fā le
上了马车，就出发了。

zǒu zhe zǒu zhe　　zuò zài chē shang de xīn niáng zi tū rán wèn gǎn chē de
走着走着，坐在车上的新娘子突然问赶车的

pú rén shuō　　biān shang de liǎng pǐ mǎ shì shéi jiā de　　pú rén huí dá
仆人说："边上的两匹马是谁家的？"仆人回答

说:"是向别人家借来的。"新娘又指着中间的马问:"这中间的马呢?"仆人又说:"是你夫家的。"新娘子说:"你若嫌车走得慢,要打就打两边的马,不要打中间的马。"驾车人听了,觉得新娘子十分自私小气。

迎亲的马车到了新郎家后,伴娘赶紧上前来扶新娘下车。谁知新媳妇一点儿也不客气,刚到夫家就以主妇的口吻吩咐伴娘说:"你平时在家做饭时,要记住一做完饭就要把灶膛里的火熄掉,以免引起火灾。"那位伴娘觉得新媳妇太多嘴了,心里很不高兴。

大家都以为新媳妇该消停了,谁知她一走进家门,看到一个石臼放在厅堂前,就立即吩咐旁边的人说:"快把这个石臼移到屋外去,别放在这里妨碍客人走路。"新娘子的行为让夫家陷入了难

kān de jìng dì　　dà jiā dōu jué de zhè ge xīn niáng zi shuō huà háo wú fēn cùn
堪的境地，大家都觉得这个新娘子说话毫无分寸，

gāng jià jìn mén jiù duì bié rén zhǐ shǒu huà jiǎo　　tài méi yǒu jiào yǎng le
刚嫁进门就对别人指手画脚，太没有教养了。

cóng nà yǐ hòu　　fū jiā rén jiù yì zhí xīn cún jiè dì　　lěng luò le xīn
从那以后，夫家人就一直心存芥蒂，冷落了新

xí fu　　qí shí　　xīn xí fu shuō de sān jiàn shì　　duì fū jiā lái shuō dōu shì
媳妇。其实，新媳妇说的三件事，对夫家来说都是

yǒu hǎo chù de　　dàn shì tā bù fēn shí jiān　　dì diǎn hé chǎng hé　　gāng tà
有好处的。但是她不分时间、地点和场合，刚踏

jìn fū jiā mén jiù yǐ zhǔ fù zì jū　　duō zuǐ duō shé　　fǎn dào yǐn qǐ le bié
进夫家门就以主妇自居，多嘴多舌，反倒引起了别

rén de bù mǎn
人的不满。

In the State of Wei, there was a family that was going to hold a wedding ceremony for their son. They had only one horse, but in order to successfully hold the wedding, they borrowed two horses from their neighbors. On the day of the wedding, the family used these three horses to pull the carriage, bustling to meet the bride. People who went to pick up the bride helped her get into the carriage and headed back home.

On the way, the bride sitting in the carriage suddenly asked her servant, "Whose horses on the both sides are they?" The servant answered, "They are borrowed from others." The bride pointed at the horse in the middle and asked again, "What about this one?" The servant said, "It belongs to your husband." The bride said, "If you think the carriage goes too slowly, you can whip the horses on both sides but don't whip the horse in the middle." When the man heard this, he thought that the bride was very stingy.

As soon as the wedding carriage arrived at the groom's family, the bridesmaid went to help the bride to get off quickly. However, the new daughter-in-law was so impolite that just after she came to the husband's family, she commanded the bridesmaid in a tone of hostess, "When you cook at home in the daily life, remember to put out fire in the hearth directly after finishing cooking lest fire disasters may happen." That bridesmaid was unhappy because she thought the new bride said too much.

Everyone thought the new daughter-in-law should stop talking, but when she walked into the house and saw a mortar placed in front of the hall, she immediately ordered the person beside her, "Hurry to move this stone mortar outside and don't put it here to hinder the guests from walking." The bride's behavior made her husband's family embarrassed. Everyone felt the bride talked without any sense of proportion for she found faults of others as soon as she entered the door.

Since then, the family was reluctant to treat the bride well. In fact, the three things mentioned by the newly-wed wife were beneficial to the husband's family. But she considered herself as hostess as soon as she entered the husband's house and made improper comments without taking the timing and situation into consideration. This made her so disagreeable.

生难字/词注解 | Note

石臼：用石头凿成的舂米谷等物的器具。

Stone mortar：A tool made of stone to husk rice and millet.

故事寓意 | The moral of the story

这个故事告诉我们：说话做事要合时宜，讲究策略和方式。如果不顾时机、不分场合地乱说话、瞎指挥，即使是好事，也得不到别人的尊重和认可，反而会惹人讥笑。

This story tells us that we should talk and behave in a proper manner with strategies. If we speak and order without paying attention to the timing and situation, even though it's a good thing, we would get teased rather than win respect and recognition from others.

夜郎自大

Arrogant Yelang People

zài hàn cháo de shí hou　xī nán biān jìng shang yǒu yí gè xiǎo guó
在汉朝的时候，西南边境上有一个小国，

míng jiào yè láng guó　lì shǔ xiàn zài wǒ guó guì zhōu ān shùn yí dài　zhè
名叫夜郎国，隶属现在我国贵州安顺一带。这

ge guó jiā hěn xiǎo　rén kǒu yě bù duō　yì zhí yǐ lái bù hé wài jiè lián
个国家很小，人口也不多，一直以来不和外界联

xì　dàn shì guó wáng què hěn jiāo ào　tā bù zhī dào wài miàn de shì jiè duō
系，但是国王却很骄傲，他不知道外面的世界多

dà　zǒng jué de zì jǐ de guó jiā jiù shì zuì dà　zuì qiáng de
大，总觉得自己的国家就是最大、最强的。

yì tiān　yè láng guó guó wáng yǔ bù xià xún shì guó jìng de shí hou
一天，夜郎国国王与部下巡视国境的时候，

tā zhǐ zhe qián fāng wèn　nǐ men kàn　zhè yí wàng wú biān de jiāng tǔ
他指着前方问："你们看！这一望无边的疆土，

dōu shì wǒ de　yǒu nǎ yì guó néng bǐ tā dà ne　bù xià men wèi le
都是我的，有哪一国能比它大呢？"部下们为了

迎合国王的心意，于是就说："当然是夜郎最大啊！"他们又来到一大片高山前，国王说："天下还找得到比这更高的山吗？"随从连忙应和说："当然找不到，天下哪有比夜郎的山更高的山呢！"

后来，他们来到河边，国王说道："你们看，这条河又宽又长，这是世界上最长最大的河了。"部下们仍然异口同声回答说："大王说得一点都没错。"从此以后，无知的国王就更相信夜郎是天底下最大的国家了。

有一次，汉朝朝廷派遣使者来到夜郎国。国王见到使者后，竟然愚昧地问道："汉朝与我们夜郎国比较，哪一个大呢？"使者听了，非常惊讶，他没有想到这样一个小小的国家，竟然能与汉朝相比，因为夜郎国和汉朝的一个县的面积差不

duō dà   tā huí dá shuō   yè láng hé hàn cháo shì wán quán bù néng xiāng
多大。他回答说："夜郎和汉朝是完全不能相

bǐ de   hàn cháo de zhōu jùn jiù yǒu hǎo jǐ shí gè   ér yè láng de quán bù
比的。汉朝的州郡就有好几十个,而夜郎的全部

dì pán hái dǐ bú shàng hàn cháo yí gè jùn de dì pán   nǐ kàn nǎ yí gè
地盘还抵不上汉朝一个郡的地盘。你看,哪一个

dà ne
大呢?"

yè láng guó wáng yì tīng bù jīn mù dèng kǒu dāi mǎn liǎn xiū kuì
夜郎国王一听,不禁目瞪口呆,满脸羞愧。

In the Han Dynasty, there was a small country on its southwestern border called Yelang which belongs to Anshun Region in Guizhou Province now. The country was very small with a small population, and it almost had no contact with other countries. The king was very arrogant and thought his country was the biggest and strongest.

One day, when the king of Yelang and his ministers patrolled along the border, he pointed forward and asked, "Look. This vast and boundless land all belongs to me. Which country is bigger than mine?" In order to please the king, his fellows all said, "Of course Yelang is the biggest!" When they came to a big mountain, the king said, "Is there any mountain higher than this?" His attendants replied instantly, "Of course not. There is no mountain higher than the mountain in Yelang!"

Later, when they came to a river, the king said, "You see, the river is wide and long. This is the longest and largest river in the world." All the ministers agreed, "It's so right for the king to say this." From then on, the ignorant king believed that his country was the largest one in the world.

Once, the Han Dynasty sent an envoy to Yelang. The king asked the envoy ignorantly, "The Han Dynasty and our country, which one is bigger?" The envoy was greatly surprised by the question. He never expected that such a small country would compare itself with the Han Dynasty because Yelang was just the same size of a small county in the Han Dynasty. He replied, "Yelang could hardly compare with Han. There are dozens of states in the Han Dynasty, while the whole territory of Yelang is smaller than one state in our country. Which country do you think is bigger?"

The king of Yelang was shocked and felt so ashamed of himself.

故事寓意 | The moral of the story

"夜郎自大"用来讽刺没有见过世面,妄自尊大的人。这个故事告诉我们:要读万卷书,行万里路,要不断地学习,不断地探索,才能知道宇宙天地的广大无边。

"Arrogant Yelang people" is used to satirize people who are arrogant because they know nothing about the world. This story tells us that we should "read ten thousand books and travel ten thousand *li*". Keep learning and exploring, and then we may know the vastness of the universe.

中　国　经　典　寓　言　故　事

第四辑

Part 4

笨人捞豆

The Stupid Man Picking Up Beans from Water

suí cháo shí hou　yǒu gè rén hěn yú dùn wú zhī　zuò shì hěn qīng shuài
隋朝时候,有个人很愚钝无知,做事很轻率,

cóng lái bù jīng tóu nǎo sī kǎo　yì tiān　tā lā le yì chē hēi dòu dào chéng
从来不经头脑思考。一天,他拉了一车黑豆到城

lǐ qù mài　lù tú yáo yuǎn　hēi dòu yòu shí fēn chén zhòng　tā fēi cháng chī
里去卖。路途遥远,黑豆又十分沉重,他非常吃

lì de lā zhe chē qián jìn　jiù zhè yàng zǒu a zǒu a　zǒu dào le yí gè
力地拉着车前进。就这样走啊走啊,走到了一个

jiào bà tóu de dì fang　tā yí bù xiǎo xīn bèi shí tou bàn dǎo le　hái niǔ
叫灞头的地方,他一不小心被石头绊倒了,还扭

shāng le jiǎo　shēn tǐ shī qù le píng héng　chē zi dǎ fān le　lǐ miàn de
伤了脚,身体失去了平衡,车子打翻了,里面的

dòu zi quán dōu sǎ chū lái le　tā jiù zhè yàng yǎn zhēng zhēng de kàn zhe yì
豆子全都洒出来了。他就这样眼睁睁地看着一

187

车黑豆全部掉进了水里。过了一会儿，他从地上爬了起来，看着水里的黑豆，不知如何是好。他想：这么多豆子，一个人要捞到什么时候啊！他决定回家叫家里人来帮忙。于是，他撇下车子和豆子就走了。

这个人刚离开，原先在周围看热闹的人就说："不知道他什么时候才能回来，这么多豆子让河水冲走了多可惜呀，不如我们把它捞回去吧。"于是大家争抢着下河去捞豆子，不一会儿，就把豆子全部捞走了。

当那个愚人回到翻车的地方时，他看见水里有许多蝌蚪在那里游来游去，以为那就是他的豆子，赶紧要下水去捞出来。可他刚一下水，蝌蚪就受到了惊吓，一下子全都游散了。这个人觉得很奇怪，呆呆地站在原地。他叹着气说："黑豆啊黑

dòu jiù suàn nǐ bú rèn shi wǒ le   lí kāi wǒ pǎo le   kě wǒ zěn me yě
豆，就 算 你 不 认 识 我 了，离 开 我 跑 了，可 我 怎 么 也

bú rèn shí nǐ le ne   nǐ zěn me hū rán jiān jiù duō chū le yì tiáo wěi
不 认 识 你 了 呢？ 你 怎 么 忽 然 间 就 多 出 了 一 条 尾

ba ya
巴 呀！"

In the Sui Dynasty，there was a stupid and ignorant person who always behaved indiscreetly. One day，he carried a cart of beans to the town to sell. Because the town was far away and the cart was loaded with black beans，the man struggled to pull the cart. He kept walking and walking，then he reached a place called Batou. He accidentally tripped over a stone and twisted his feet，then his body lost balance and the cart tilted over. The black beans all spilled out and he just kept on watching a whole cart of black beans fall into the water. After a while，he stood up，watching the black beans in the water helplessly，not knowing what to do. He thought it would take a long time to get all the beans back just by himself. So he decided to go home and asked his family for help. So he left the cart and beans there.

As soon as the man walked away，people who just gathered there said，"We do not know when he would come back and it is too pitiful to let so many beans be washed away by the water. Let us take them back from the water." So they scrambled to get the beans, and soon all the beans were taken away.

The stupid man came back to the place where the cart tilted over. He saw a lot of polliwogs in the water swimming around and mistook them for his beans. He hurried to go down in the water, but the polliwogs were frightened to swim away instantly. The man felt strange and stood there dully. He sighed to himself and said, "Black beans, you couldn't recognize me and left me, but how could I not know you? How do you suddenly have a tail?"

故事寓意 | The moral of the story

　　故事中的"笨人"想当然地做事情,结果无法判断事情的真相。这个故事告诉我们:做事要经过头脑思考,不要随意地下判断,做决定。

　　The "stupid man" in the story just did things mechanically without thinking, and this makes it impossible for him to make the right judgment. The story tells us that we need to think prudently before making judgments and decisions.

对牛弹琴

Playing the Zither in Front of the Cows

chūn qiū shí qī　　lǔ guó yǒu yí gè zhù míng de yīn yuè jiā　míng jiào
春秋时期，鲁国有一个著名的音乐家，名叫

gōng míng yí　　tā fēi cháng shàn yú tán qín　　rén men cóng tā de qín shēng
公明仪，他非常善于弹琴。人们从他的琴声

zhōng néng tīng de chū chán chán de liú shuǐ shēng　　dà hǎi xiōng yǒng de làng tāo
中能听得出潺潺的流水声，大海汹涌的浪涛

shēng　　hái néng tīng chū qiū chóng jī jī de dī míng　　xiǎo niǎo wǎn zhuǎn de gē
声；还能听出秋虫唧唧的低鸣、小鸟婉转的歌

chàng　　qū diào huān kuài shí　　huì ràng rén jīn bú zhù méi kāi yǎn xiào　qū diào
唱。曲调欢快时，会让人禁不住眉开眼笑；曲调

bēi āi shí　　néng shǐ rén xīn suān bù yǐ　　gēn zhe qín shēng yì qǐ shāng xīn liú
悲哀时，能使人心酸不已，跟着琴声一起伤心流

lèi　　fán shì tīng guò tā tán qín de rén　　dōu bèi tā de qín shēng gǎn dòng
泪。凡是听过他弹琴的人，都被他的琴声感动。

yí cì　　tā dài zhe qín dào jiāo wài sàn bù　　kàn dào yǒu jǐ tóu niú zài
一次，他带着琴到郊外散步，看到有几头牛在

tián yě lǐ chī cǎo　　xīn xiǎng　　wǒ de qín shēng　　tīng le de rén dōu shuō
田野里吃草，心想："我的琴声，听了的人都说

好，牛会不会也觉得好呢？让我来试一试。"于是，

他坐到牛的旁边，对着牛弹了一段高雅优美的曲

子。这琴声果然非常美妙动听，任何人听了都

会忍不住地夸赞。可是那些牛还是静静地低着头

吃它们的草，丝毫没有反应，就好像它们从来不

曾听到过什么一样。

公明仪看见美妙的琴声并不能打动牛，十

分气恼。过了一会儿，他想出一个办法。只见他

抚动琴弦，弹出一段段奇怪杂乱的声音，有的

像嗡嗡的蚊蝇声，有的像迷路的小牛犊发出

的叫声。这时候那些大公牛才像突然明白了什

么似的，总算有反应了，它们竖起耳朵、甩着尾

巴，迈着小步子走来走去地倾听着琴声。

During the Spring and Autumn period, in the State of Lu there was a musician named Gongming Yi who played musical instruments very well. From his performance, you could hear the gurgling sound of flowing water, the rough sea waves and chirp of insects in autumn and birds' melodious singing. Hearing his cheerful melodies, people couldn't help smiling, while his sad tunes made people shed tears sorrowfully. Anyone who had listened to his performance would be moved.

One day, Gongming Yi saw several cows eating grass when he was having a walk in the countryside with his ancient Chinese zither. He thought, "Everybody compliments my music. How would the cows feel?" So he played a piece of elegant music for the cows, hoping they could appreciate it, but the cows just kept grazing the grass with their heads down, as if nothing happened.

Gongming Yi was annoyed by the cows' lack of response but then he had a good idea. He played in a way that sounded like the sound of mosquitos and the moo of calves. The cows finally seemed to understand it and responded, cocking their ears and shaking their tails. They listened to the music wholeheartedly while walking around.

故事寓意 | **The moral of the story**

"对牛弹琴"比喻说话不看对象，或对外行人讲深刻的道理，纯粹是白费口舌。这个故事告诉我们：说话、做事要看清楚对象，根据事物的不同特点，有针对性地思考解决方法，这样才能够达到预期效果。

"Playing the zither in front of the cows" means that it's a waste to speak if we are not mindful of our listeners and do not talk to them in a way they can understand. This story tells us that we should be clear about the target when we're talking or taking action. We should find solutions according to different characteristics of things, so as to achieve the expected result.

狐假虎威

The Fox Assuming the Majesty of the Tiger

lǎo hǔ hào chēng　bǎi shòu zhī wáng　　sēn lín zhōng suǒ yǒu de dòng wù
老虎号称"百兽之王",森林中所有的动物

dōu hěn hài pà tā　lǎo hǔ fēi cháng dé yì　　yǒu yì tiān　yì zhī lǎo hǔ
都很害怕它,老虎非常得意。有一天,一只老虎

zhèng zài sēn lín lǐ wán shuǎ　tū rán kàn jiàn le　yì zhī hú li　　tā xùn sù
正在森林里玩耍,突然看见了一只狐狸。它迅速

de zhuō zhù hú li　　xīn xiǎng jīn tiān yòu kě　yǐ měi měi de xiǎng shòu yí dùn
地捉住狐狸,心想今天又可以美美地享受一顿

wǔ cān le
午餐了。

hú li shēng xìng jiǎo huá　tā zhī dào bèi lǎo hǔ zhuō zhù le　bì sǐ wú
狐狸生性狡猾,它知道被老虎捉住了必死无

yí　　tā hěn zháo jí　　jiù xiǎng chū le yí gè bàn fǎ　tā duì lǎo hǔ shuō
疑。它很着急,就想出了一个办法,它对老虎说:

nǐ bù néng chī wǒ　wǒ shì tiān dì pài lái tǒng zhì bǎi shòu de　nǐ yào shì
"你不能吃我,我是天帝派来统治百兽的,你要是

chī le wǒ　tiān dì kěn dìng huì chéng fá nǐ de　　lǎo hǔ duì hú li de huà
吃了我,天帝肯定会惩罚你的。"老虎对狐狸的话

很怀疑，就问道："你当百兽之王，有什么可以证明？"狐狸连忙说："你如果不相信我的话，可以跟随我到森林中去走一走，让你亲眼看看百兽见了我是不是都很害怕。"老虎听说后，心想这也是个办法，反正狐狸在它手上肯定是跑不掉的。于是它就让狐狸在前面带路，它跟随在狐狸的后面，一起走进山林的深处。

森林中的动物们看见老虎来了，一个个很惊慌，纷纷夺路逃命。转了一圈之后，狐狸扬扬得意地对老虎说道："现在你该看到了吧？森林中的百兽，有谁敢不怕我？"老虎不知道那些动物害怕的是它自己，听到狐狸这样说，只好把它放走了。

The tiger is known as the "king of beasts" and all animals are afraid of it very much. One day, the tiger was playing in the forest and suddenly he saw a fox. The tiger quickly caught the fox and thought he would have a nice lunch.

The fox was cunning, and it knew that it would definitely die when got caught by the tiger. It was scared and soon came up with an idea. The fox said to the tiger, "You can't eat me. I am sent by the Lord of Heaven to rule the animals. If you eat me, you will be punished by the Lord of Heaven." The tiger was very suspicious of the fox's words, so he asked, "How can you prove it?" The fox said quickly, "If you don't believe me, just follow me to the forest and see whether all the animals are afraid of me." After hearing this, the tiger thought it might be a good idea because there was no possibility that the fox could escape. So the tiger let the fox lead the way into the mountains and followed the fox.

When the animals in the forest saw the tiger coming, they were all frightened and ran away. After they had walked around, the fox said to the tiger with an air of exultation, "Now you've seen that. Among all the beasts in the forest, who is not afraid of me?" The tiger did not know that the animal was afraid of himself and had to let go of the fox.

故事寓意 | The moral of the story

"狐假虎威"用来比喻倚仗别人的势力去欺负人或恐吓人。这个故事告诉我们：在生活中对于那些像狐狸一样仗势欺人的人，我们不要害怕，应该学会识破他们的伎俩。

"The fox assuming the majesty of the tiger" is used to describe people who bully or frighten others by relying on others' power. This story tells us that when confronting people bullying us like the fox, we don't need to be afraid, and instead we should learn to see through their tricks.

画蛇添足

Adding Feet to the Drawing of a Snake

zhàn guó shí qī yǒu gè chǔ guó rén guò jié de shí hou jì sì zǔ xiān
战国时期，有个楚国人过节的时候祭祀祖先，

yí shì jié shù hòu tā ná chū yì hú jiǔ shǎng cì gěi pú rén men hē yīn
仪式结束后，他拿出一壶酒赏赐给仆人们喝。因

wèi rén hěn duō zhè hú jiǔ rú guǒ gěi dà jiā hē shì bú gòu de hái bù rú
为人很多，这壶酒如果给大家喝是不够的，还不如

gān cuì gěi yí gè rén hē ràng tā hē gè tòng kuài
干脆给一个人喝，让他喝个痛快。

kě shì gěi nǎ ge rén hē ne zhè shí yǒu rón jiàn yì shuō měi gè
可是给哪个人喝呢？这时有人建议说："每个

rén zài dì shang huà yì tiáo shé shéi huà de kuài yòu huà de hǎo jiù bǎ zhè
人在地上画一条蛇，谁画得快又画得好，就把这

hú jiǔ gěi tā hē dà jiā rèn wéi zhè ge bàn fǎ hǎo dōu tóng yì zhè yàng
壶酒给他喝。"大家认为这个办法好，都同意这样

zuò yú shì dà jiā zài dì shang kāi shǐ huà qǐ lái yǒu gè rén huà de
做。于是，大家在地上开始画起来。有个人画得

hěn kuài yì zhuǎn yǎn zuì xiān huà hǎo le tā jiù duān qǐ jiǔ hú yào hē jiǔ
很快，一转眼最先画好了，他就端起酒壶要喝酒，

kě shì tā zhuǎn shēn kàn kan bié rén hái méi yǒu huà hǎo ne tā shí fēn dé
可是他转身看看别人，还没有画好呢，他十分得

yì shuō nǐ men zhè me màn wǒ zài gěi shé tiān shàng jǐ zhī jiǎo nǐ
意，说："你们这么慢，我再给蛇添上几只脚，你

men yě bù yí dìng néng gòu huà wán shuō zhe jiù gěi shé huà shàng le jǐ
们也不一定能够画完。"说着，就给蛇画上了几

zhī jiǎo
只脚。

zhè shí lìng wài yí gè rén yě huà hǎo le jiù qiǎng guò jiǔ hú shuō
这时，另外一个人也画好了，就抢过酒壶说：

shé shì méi yǒu jiǎo de nǐ wèi shén me yào gěi tā tiān shàng jiǎo ne shuō
"蛇是没有脚的，你为什么要给它添上脚呢？"说

wán jiù yǎng qǐ tóu lái gū lū gū lū jǐ kǒu bǎ jiǔ hē wán le nà ge gěi
完就仰起头来，咕噜咕噜几口把酒喝完了，那个给

shé huà jiǎo de rén shí fēn hòu huǐ
蛇画脚的人十分后悔。

During the Warring States period, after the ceremony of worshipping their ancestors, a man from the State of Chu gave a pot of wine as a reward to his servants. Obviously there were too many servants and only one pot of wine wasn't sufficient for all of them, and it would be much better if the wine was given to one person.

But who should have it? Then someone suggested, "Everyone shall draw a snake on the ground, and the one that finishes drawing first will win the pot of wine." They all thought it was a good idea and agreed. Therefore, everybody squatted on the ground and began to draw a snake. One of them finished drawing quickly, then he took the pot and was about to drink. When he looked around at others who had not finished yet, he said contemptuously, "How slowly you all are. I still have time to add feet to the snake before you finish it." Then he started to add feet to the snake.

Right at that moment, another man finished and then snatched the pot and said, "Snakes have no feet. Why do you add feet to it?" Then he drank the wine. The person who added feet to the snake felt very regretful.

生难字/词注解 | Note

祭祀： 置备供品对神佛或祖先行礼，表示崇敬并祈求保佑。

Ceremony of worshipping： Sacrifice something that is valuable in a special religious ceremony as an offering to the gods or ancestors.

故事寓意 | The moral of the story

"画蛇添足"比喻有的人自以为是，喜欢多此一举，结果往往弄巧成拙。这个故事告诉我们：做任何事情都要实事求是，不要卖弄小聪明，做出多余或不妥当的事情。

"Adding feet to the drawing of a snake" satirizes that some people are arrogant and do things superfluously which turn out to be stupid instead. The story tells us that we must be realistic and not overreach ourselves by doing unnecessary or inappropriate things.

囫囵吞枣

Swallowing a Date Whole

从前，有个人看书的时候，总是会大声朗读，可是他从来不去思考书中的意思，还自以为看了很多书，懂得许多道理。

一天，他参加朋友的聚会，大家边吃边聊，其中有一位客人感慨地说："这世上很少有两全其美的事，就拿吃水果来说，梨对牙齿很好，但是吃多了伤胃；吃枣呢，正好与吃梨相反，吃枣子能健胃，可惜吃多了会伤牙齿。"

那个读书不求甚解的人为了表现自己的聪明，就说："我有一个好主意，可以吃梨有利牙齿又不伤脾，吃枣健脾又不至于伤牙齿。"大家都很感兴趣，就问他有什么办法。他慢吞吞地说："这很简单嘛！吃梨时，我只是用牙齿去嚼，却不吞咽下去，它就伤不着脾胃了；吃枣时，我就不用嚼了，一口吞咽下去，这样就不会伤到牙齿了。"有个喜欢开玩笑的人说："你这不是将枣整个吞下去了吗？"

大家听了，都哈哈大笑起来。原来是这个年轻人自作聪明，如果按他说的办法，将枣子整个地连核一起吞下去了，就会难以消化，哪里还谈得上什么健脾胃呢？所以，大家才讥笑他。

Once upon a time, there was a man who always read books out loud without thinking about the meanings in them. He felt that he knew a lot since he had read many books.

One day, in a gathering, when they were just eating and chatting, one guest said, "It's impossible to keep the cake while eating it. Take fruits for example. The pear is good for teeth but too many will be bad for the stomach. The date has the function of nourishing the spleen and stomach, but eating too many dates will be bad for the teeth."

The young man who was content with a superficial understanding tried to show off, so he said, "I have a good idea." People were interested and asked how, and he replied slowly, "It's quite simple. When eating pears, I only chew them with my teeth, and spit them out instead of swallowing them. And when eating dates, I swallow them whole instead of chewing them." Someone teased him, "You can really swallow a date whole?"

After hearing this, everybody present laughed at the young man's stupid idea. If people ate the date whole as he suggested, there would be digestion problems. How could it even be good for the spleen and stomach? That's why all the people around laughed at him.

故事寓意 | The moral of the story

　　"囫囵吞枣"比喻学习或理解事情不加分析研究，笼统地接受。这个故事告诉我们：学习知识时不能一味地生吞活剥，不加细致地分析、理解。因为笼统接受只能是浮光掠影，肤浅理解，那是没有什么收获的，也学不到真正的知识。

　　"Swallowing a date whole" is used to describe people who learn things hastily without thinking or accept the whole fact without distinction. The story tells us that when we are absorbing knowledge, we should not swallow the whole information without analyzing and understanding. Gulping down the whole, you could just get the superficial understanding and you'll never get the useful knowledge.

书呆子赶鸡

The Bookworm Shooing the Chickens

cóng qián yǒu gè shū dāi zi zhǐ huì mēn zhe tóu dú shū shén me shì
从前，有个书呆子，只会闷着头读书，什么事

yě bú huì gàn yǒu yì tiān bàng wǎn tā de qī zi cóng wài miàn gàn huó huí
也不会干。有一天傍晚，他的妻子从外面干活回

jiā kàn dào jiā lǐ yǎng de jī méi yǒu huí lái jiù duì tā shuō wǒ xiàn
家，看到家里养的鸡没有回来，就对他说："我现

zài yào zuò fàn nǐ qù bāng wǒ bǎ jī dōu gǎn jìn wō qù ba shū dāi zi
在要做饭，你去帮我把鸡都赶进窝去吧。"书呆子

dā ying le tā fàng xià shǒu lǐ de shū pǎo dào wài miàn yuàn zi qù tā
答应了，他放下手里的书，跑到外面院子去。他

yí kàn dào jiā lǐ de jǐ zhī jī lián máng shàng qù shǐ jìn gǎn jié guǒ bǎ
一看到家里的几只鸡，连忙上去使劲赶，结果把

nà jǐ zhī jī xià de luàn fēi luàn cuàn
那几只鸡吓得乱飞乱窜。

shū dāi zi zhǐ hǎo zhàn zài nà lǐ bù gǎn luàn dòng nà jǐ zhī jī
书呆子只好站在那里，不敢乱动。那几只鸡

màn màn de ān jìng xià lái　　xiàng yuàn zi běi bian zǒu qù　　shū dāi zi gǎn máng
慢慢地安静下来，向院子北边走去，书呆子赶忙

shàng qián jiāng jī lán zhù　　　jī xià de cháo nán bian pǎo qù　　shū dāi zi yòu
上前将鸡拦住。鸡吓得朝南边跑去，书呆子又

shàng qián qù zǔ lán　　jī yòu chóng xīn cháo běi bian pǎo qù　　　jiù zhè yàng lái
上前去阻拦，鸡又重新朝北边跑去。就这样来

huí de zhuī gǎn　　shū dāi zi　shǐ zhōng dōu méi yǒu chéng gōng
回地追赶，书呆子始终都没有成功。

　　tiān sè　yǐ jīng hěn wǎn le　　qī zi zuò hǎo le fàn　　hái bú jiàn zhàng fu
天色已经很晚了，妻子做好了饭，还不见丈夫

gǎn jī huí jiā　　yú shì　tā chū mén chá kàn　　fā xiàn shū dāi zi zhèng shǎ
赶鸡回家。于是，她出门查看，发现书呆子正傻

shǎ de zhàn zài nà lǐ　　qī zi hěn shēng qì　　gào su tā gǎn jī　yě yào yǒu
傻地站在那里。妻子很生气，告诉他赶鸡也要有

fāng fǎ　　yīng gāi zài jī ān jìng de shí hou màn màn kào jìn tā　　rú guǒ tā
方法："应该在鸡安静的时候慢慢靠近它。如果它

jīng huāng　nǐ jiù sǎ diǎn gǔ zi qù màn màn yǐn yòu tā men guò lái　　jǐn liàng
惊慌，你就撒点谷子去慢慢引诱它们过来，尽量

bǎ jī gǎn dào shú xi de lù shang　　tā zì rán ér rán jiù huì huí wō le
把鸡赶到熟悉的路上，它自然而然就会回窝了。"

shū dāi zi huǎng rán dà wù　　shuō　　xiǎng bú dào gǎn jī yě yǒu xué wèn　zěn
书呆子恍然大悟，说："想不到赶鸡也有学问，怎

me shū běn shang jiù jiàn bú dào ne
么书本上就见不到呢？"

Once upon a time, there was a bookworm who just read books and was not able to do anything else. One day at dusk, his wife came back from working and found chickens were still outside, so she said to him, "I'm going to prepare dinner, and please help me to shoo all the chickens to the nest." The bookworm agreed.

He put down his book and went into the yard. He hurried up and tried to shoo the chickens, but the chickens just scurried and flew all around. The bookworm could do nothing and dared not to move. The chickens gradually calmed down and walked toward the northern corner of the yard. The bookworm hurried to shoo them, but the chickens were frightened and then ran to the southern corner then. And the man again tried to shoo them, but the chickens ran away to the north. He ran and chased like this for many times but all failed.

It became quite dark and the wife had already finished cooking the dinner, but the husband still wasn't back. So she went out to check and just found the bookworm standing there like a fool. The wife was very angry and told him that there was a skill in shooing the chickens, "You should try to get close to them when they're quiet. Then you drop a little bit of millet to lure them into the path they are familiar with. Finally they would return to the nest by themselves." The bookworm was suddenly struck by the meaning of the situation and said, "There is even a kind of skill in shooing the chickens. Why have I never learned this from books?"

故事寓意 | The moral of the story

"书呆子"是指只会死读书，对书本以外的东西一无所知的人。这个故事告诉我们：做任何事情都有它的规律和方法，如果不讲究方式方法，想当然地胡来蛮干，是很难把事情做好的。

"Bookworm" refers to a person who just reads books and knows nothing of the world outside the books. The story tells us that there are routines and methods in doing everything. Doing things just in accordance with imagination recklessly without following rules, we could hardly handle things well.

秀才的"大志"

The Scholars'"Ambition"

gǔ shí hou   yǒu liǎng gè shí fēn lǎn duò de xiù cai   tā men zhěng tiān
古时候，有两个十分懒惰的秀才，他们 整天

tān tú xiǎng lè   jǐn guǎn tā men de shēng huó shí fēn jié jū   chuān de yī
贪图享乐。尽管他们的 生活十分拮据，穿的衣

fu yòu jiù yòu pò   hái jīng cháng chī bù bǎo fàn   kě shì tā men réng rán bú
服又旧又破，还经 常 吃不饱饭。可是他们仍然不

qù gàn huó   jiù zhī dào zhuāng mú zuò yàng   jué de zì jǐ mǎn fù cái xué
去干活，就知道 装 模作样，觉得自己满腹才学，

wú suǒ bú zhī
无所不知。

yì tiān   zhè liǎng gè xiù cai jù dào le yì qǐ   tā men zuò zài yí gè
一天，这两个秀才聚到了一起。他们坐在一个

dà shù dūn shang   shǒu lǐ ná zhe yì bǎ pò jiù de dà shàn zi   bù tíng de
大树墩上，手里拿着一把破旧的大扇子，不停地

yáo zhe shàn zi   qū gǎn zhe wén chóng   tā men kàn jiàn nóng rén zài tián dì
摇着扇子，驱赶着蚊 虫。他们看见农人在田地

里辛苦地干活,汗流浃背,衣服都湿了,觉得十分辛苦。两个秀才摇了摇头,一副不屑的样子。其中一个秀才说:"他们真苦啊!这么苦这么累,能得到什么呢?虽说我这一辈子穷是穷了点儿,可是我只要吃饱了饭,睡足了觉也就可以了。我最讨厌的就是像他们这样下地干活,他们一个个真是目光短浅,胸无大志呀!如果将来有一天我的理想实现了,我一定先把肚子吃得饱饱的,再睡个好觉;睡够了再起来吃,吃了又继续睡,如果真的是这样那该多有福气呀!有了这样的福气,我这一生就别无他求了,也算是实现我的'大志'了。你说是这样吗?"

另一个秀才不同意前一个秀才的观点。他说:"我跟你可不一样啊。我的原则是吃饱了还要再吃,哪有时间去睡觉呀!我要不停地吃,不停

de chī zhè cái shì rén shì jiān zuì dà de lè qù　zhè cái shì wǒ de　dà
地吃，这才是人世间最大的乐趣。这才是我的'大

zhì　ne
志'呢！"

liǎng gè xiù cai jiù zhè yàng zhěng tiān zuò zhe tán lùn tā men de　dà
两个秀才就这样整天坐着谈论他们的"大

zhì　què cóng wèi fù zhū háng dòng　jiù zhè yàng　duō shao nián guò qù le
志"，却从未付诸行动。就这样，多少年过去了，

tā men de shēng huó yī jiù pín kǔ kùn dùn
他们的生活依旧贫苦困顿。

In ancient times, there were two lazy scholars who did nothing but sought pleasure every day. Though they lived in penury, wearing shabby and ragged clothes and often starving, they did nothing but acted as if they were talented and knew everything.

One day, the two scholars gathered together. They sat on a big tree stump with big old fans in their hands. As the insects were too annoying, they had to keep waving the fan to drive them away. Then they saw some peasants working hard in the field with their clothes soaked with sweat. Reflecting how tiring this could be, they shook their heads and put on airs of arrogance. One man uttered, "How tired they must be! What on earth, I wonder, could they gain from working so hard and bitterly? It's true that I lead a poor life，but as long as I can eat my full meals and get enough sleep，it'll be OK for me. What I hate is to work like those who are short-sighted and aimless. Should my dream come true one day，I would be sure to eat well and have a tight sleep，then wake up to eat and continue to sleep. What a blessing it is. Were this to happen，I would totally be blessed and have nothing more to desire—this is my great ambition realized. Don't you think so?"

The other one didn't agree with him. He argued，"Mine is absolutely different from yours. My rule is to keep eating even if you are already full，and how can you find time to sleep with all your time occupied in eating? I will keep eating and eating，and it is the most pleasant thing in the world. Eating all the delicious food without stop is the greatest pleasure in the world. And this is my great ambition."

In this case，the two scholars just sat around talking about their ambitions but did nothing to make it real. Years passed，and they still had to struggle financially. Dreaming without action makes great ambition vanish like bubbles.

故事寓意 | The moral of the story

两秀才所谓的"大志"，仅仅只是满足口腹之欲，这是人类最低级的生活欲求，却被他们当作远大的理想来信奉，实在是既可悲又可笑。这个故事告诉我们：人应该树立起有责任感的远大志向，为人类的福祉和社会的进步贡献自己的力量。

The so called "ambition" of these two scholars is simply all about satisfying their physical needs, which is the lowest level of human desire. It's rather pathetic and hilarious to treat the lust for food as an ideal. It informs us that one should set up a lofty goal and take over the responsibility of making a contribution to the happiness of mankind and the progress of society.

叶公好龙

Lord Ye Loves the Dragon

春秋时期，楚国有一个人，名叫叶公。他经常对别人说："我特别喜欢龙，你瞧，龙多么神气、多么吉祥啊！"于是，当他家装修房子的时候，工匠们就帮他在房梁、柱子、门窗、墙壁上到处都雕刻一条条巨龙的形象。就连穿的衣服、盖的被子、挂的蚊帐也都绣上了活灵活现的龙。

叶公这样喜爱龙，被天上的真龙知道后，

真龙非常感动。真龙想："没想到人间还有一个这样喜欢我的人呢！我得下去看看他。"

一天，真龙就从天宫来到叶公的家里。真龙把大大的头搭在叶公家的窗台上，把长长的身子盘在叶公家客堂的柱子上，尾巴就伸到了厅堂里。叶公在卧室听到有异样的声音，就走出来看，一看到真龙，叶公顿时吓得脸色苍白，浑身发抖，大叫一声逃走了。真龙感到莫名其妙，很是失望。其实叶公并不是真的喜欢龙，他喜欢的只不过是那些像龙的东西而已。

In the Spring and Autumn period, in the State of Chu there was a man called Lord Ye who always told others, "I am extremely fond of the dragon. Look, how powerful and auspicious it is!" So when he decorated his house, he had the craftsmen carve giant dragons on the beams, pillars, doors, windows and walls of his house. Even his clothes, quilts, mosquito nets were embroidered with vivid dragons.

The real dragon in the heaven was greatly moved by Lord Ye's love for him. The dragon thought, "I couldn't imagine that there is such a person who has such a strong affection for me on the earth. I must go down and visit him."

So one day, the real dragon came down from the heaven to Lord Ye's house. The dragon turned its giant head through the window of Lord Ye, and left its body winding around the pillar and its long tail in the sitting room. Lord Ye in the bedroom heard some noise and came out. Seeing the real dragon, Lord Ye was terrified and his face turned pale. He couldn't help trembling and shouted in horror, and then escaped. The real dragon felt baffled and disappointed. It turned out that Lord Ye was just fond of dragon-like things instead of the real dragon.

故事寓意 | The moral of the story

"叶公好龙"用来形容那些表面上喜欢某种事物,其实心里并不是真正喜欢的人。这个故事告诉我们:要实事求是,真诚待人,只有这样我们才能言行一致,心安理得,不会为了那些虚名所累。

"Lord Ye loves the dragon" is used to describe those who seem to go in for something but not actually like it from the bottom of the heart. This story tells us that we should be realistic and sincere. Only in this way can we suit our actions to our words and live peacefully without being bothered by underserved reputation.

一枕美梦

A Fond Dream

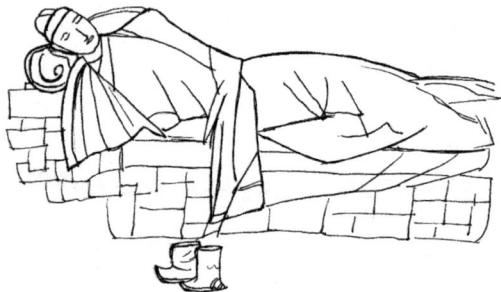

gǔ shí hou　　yǒu yí zuò jiāo hú miào　　miào lǐ yǒu yí gè yù zhěn tou
古时候，有一座焦湖庙，庙里有一个玉枕头，

zhěn tou shang yǒu yí gè xiǎo kǒng　　chuán shuō　　zhěn zhe zhè ge zhěn tou shuì
枕头上有一个小孔。传说，枕着这个枕头睡

jiào　kě yǐ zài mèng lǐ jīng lì xǔ duō měi hǎo de shì qing　　yǒu gè míng jiào
觉，可以在梦里经历许多美好的事情。有个名叫

yáng lín de rén　　píng shí zuò diǎn xiǎo shēng yì　　shēng huó jiǒng pò　　yīn cǐ
杨林的人，平时做点小生意，生活窘迫，因此

zhěng tiān dōu hěn fán mèn　　yì tiān　yáng lín tiāo zhe chén zhòng de huò wù qù
整天都很烦闷。一天，杨林挑着沉重的货物去

fàn mài　　zǒu de mǎn tóu dà hàn　gāng hǎo jīng guò jiāo hú miào　jiù dǎ suàn jìn
贩卖，走得满头大汗，刚好经过焦湖庙，就打算进

qù xiū xi yí xià　　yáng lín guì zài pú sà gēn qián qí dǎo　shuō　　bǎo yòu
去休息一下。杨林跪在菩萨跟前祈祷，说："保佑

wǒ néng yǒu hǎo yùn qi　　guò shàng xìng fú kuài lè de shēng huó
我能有好运气，过上幸福快乐的生活！"

庙里有一个巫师看见杨林十分虔诚,就拿出那个神奇的玉枕头给杨林,说道:"你先去睡一会儿吧。"杨林枕着玉枕头睡着了,他做了一个梦,梦见自己来到一户大富大贵的人家,户主是地位显赫的官员赵太尉,他做了赵太尉的女婿,他自己也升官发财了。妻子美丽、温柔,还生下了六个儿子。杨林有享受不尽的荣华富贵。他无忧无虑地生活着。一转眼几十年过去了,他还是一点都不想回家。

忽然,杨林一觉醒来,发现自己还睡在寺庙里,头枕在玉枕头上,梦中美好的一切都不见了,只有身边没有卖完的货物还堆在原地,心中禁不住十分惆怅。

In ancient times, there was a temple called Jiaohu, and in the temple there was a jade pillow with a tiny hole. It is said that sleeping on the pillow could make you dream many wonderful things. A man called Yang Lin did small business and made little money, and he was very fretful and bored all day long.

One day, Yang Lin carried a heavy load of goods to sell, sweating all over his face. He came to Jiaohu Temple and decided to take a rest there. He prayed in front of the Buddha, "God bless me with good luck and a happy life." A sorcerer in the temple happened to see Yang Lin so pious, and he gave the magic jade pillow to Yang Lin, and said, "You go rest for a while." Yang Lin slept on the pillow and began to dream.

He dreamt that he came to a large well-off family owned by the prominent official Zhao in charge of military affairs. He became the son-in-law of the family and got promotions and prosperity. His beautiful wife gave birth to six sons. He lived a carefree life with abundant wealth and great honor. Dozens of years passed quickly, but he still didn't want to go back home.

Suddenly Yang Lin woke up to find himself sleeping on the jade pillow inside the temple. All the splendid things in the dream were gone, with only the goods piled at the same place. He couldn't help feeling a sense of loss.

故事寓意 | The moral of the story

这个故事告诉我们：美满幸福的生活，不是从虚幻的白日梦中得来的。我们任何时候都不要指望坐享其成，只有通过勤恳地劳动，才能把美好的愿望变成现实。

This story tells us that we can't obtain a happy life through daydreaming, and at no time should we expect to enjoy fruits of others' work. We could only turn good wishes into reality through hard work.

揠苗助长

To Help the Crops Grow by Pulling Them Upward

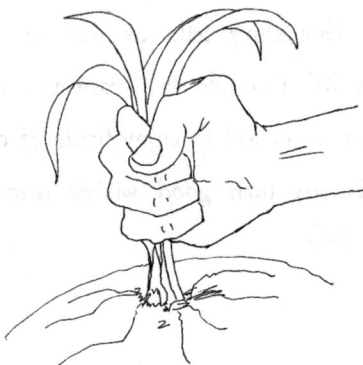

chūn qiū shí qī　sòng guó yǒu gè nóng fū　xìng gé hěn jí zào　zuò shì
春秋时期，宋国有个农夫，性格很急躁，做事

bù jīng tóu nǎo sī kǎo　hěn qīng shuài xíng shì　tā zhòng dì　kàn dào zì jǐ
不经头脑思考，很轻率行事。他种地，看到自己

tián lǐ de hé miáo zhǎng de tài màn　jiù tiān tiān zài tián jiān dì tóu zǒu lái zǒu
田里的禾苗长得太慢，就天天在田间地头走来走

qù　kě shì　yì tiān　liǎng tiān　sān tiān　hé miáo hǎo xiàng yì diǎn yě méi
去。可是，一天、两天、三天，禾苗好像一点也没

yǒu zhǎng gāo　tā xīn lǐ hěn zháo jí　zì yán zì yǔ　wǒ děi xiǎng gè
有长高。他心里很着急，自言自语："我得想个

bàn fǎ bāng zhù tā men zhǎng gāo
办法帮助它们长高"。

yì tiān　tā zhōng yú xiǎng dào le bàn fǎ　zhǐ jiàn tā jí jí máng
一天，他终于想到了办法。只见他急急忙

máng de pǎo dào tián lǐ　bǎ hé miáo yì kē kē wǎng shàng bá gāo yí duàn
忙地跑到田里，把禾苗一棵棵往上拔高一段。

cóng zhōng wǔ yì zhí máng dào tài yáng luò shān bǎ tā lèi huài le kě shì
从 中 午 一 直 忙 到 太 阳 落 山 ，把 他 累 坏 了 ，可 是

tā què hěn gāo xìng
他 却 很 高 兴 。

rán hòu tā tuō zhe pí bèi de shēn tǐ huí dào le jiā dào jiā hòu
然 后 ，他 拖 着 疲 惫 的 身 体 回 到 了 家 。 到 家 后 ，

tā yì biān chuǎn qì yì biān dà shēng de duì jiā lǐ rén shuō jīn tiān wǒ lèi
他 一 边 喘 气 一 边 大 声 地 对 家 里 人 说 ："今 天 我 累

huài le lì qi zǒng suàn méi bái fèi hé miáo dōu zhǎng gāo le yí dà jié
坏 了 ，力 气 总 算 没 白 费 ，禾 苗 都 长 高 了 一 大 截 。"

jiā lǐ rén tīng le gǎn máng pǎo dào tián lǐ qù kàn fā xiàn hé miáo quán dōu
家 里 人 听 了 ，赶 忙 跑 到 田 里 去 看 ，发 现 禾 苗 全 都

kū sǐ le
枯 死 了 。

In the State of Song during the Spring and Autumn period，
there was a farmer of quick temper who always did things
imprudently. He found that his crops grow too slowly and worried
a lot，so he walked around his field every day. Many days
passed，but it seemed that the seedlings hadn't grown higher. He
was impatient and murmured to himself, "I must find a way to help
them grow faster."

One day，he finally came up with a solution. He dashed to
the field and started to pull the crops up one by one from the early
morning to the sunset. He was extremely exhausted but satisfied.

Then he went back home with a tired body. After reaching home, he gasped to his family, "I was completely tired today, but I didn't beat the air. I helped the crops grow a little bit higher." After listening to his words, his family rushed to the field only to find all of the crops were dead.

生难字/词注解 | Note

揠：拔。

Pull：Hold something firmly and use force in order to move it away from its previous position.

故事寓意 | The moral of the story

"揠苗助长"用来比喻不顾及事物发展的规律，急于求成，结果反而把事情弄糟糕。这个故事告诉我们：要遵循事物发展规律，不能蛮干，过分在乎结果，往往会得不偿失。

"To help the crops grow by pulling them upward" is used to satirize people who are too eager to get things done only make things worse by neglecting the natural rules. The story tells us that we should follow the rules instead of rushing headlong into things. Caring too much about the result may lead to greater loss.

朝三暮四

Three in the Morning and Four in the Evening

chūn qiū shí qī　sòng guó yǒu yí gè jiào jū gōng de rén　zài jiā lǐ
春秋时期，宋国有一个叫狙公的人，在家里

yǎng le yí dà qún hóu zi　xiāng chǔ jiǔ le　jū gōng duì hóu zi de shēng
养了一大群猴子。相处久了，狙公对猴子的生

huó xí xìng yǔ xíng wéi wán quán liǎo jiě　zhè xiē hóu zi yě dōu néng gòu tīng
活习性与行为完全了解，这些猴子也都能够听

dǒng zhǔ rén de huà
懂主人的话。

　　jū gōng yǎng de hóu zi tài duō　měi tiān yào chī diào dà liàng shí wù
　　狙公养的猴子太多，每天要吃掉大量食物，

ér tā de jiā tíng bìng bù fù yù　zhè shǐ jū gōng hěn wéi nán　yú shì　tā
而他的家庭并不富裕，这使狙公很为难。于是，他

xiǎng xiàn zhì yí xià hóu zi měi tiān chī de shí wù liàng　jū gōng jiā mén kǒu
想限制一下猴子每天吃的食物量。狙公家门口

zhǎng le yì kē gāo dà mào shèng de xiàng shù shù shang jié mǎn le hóu zi
长了一棵高大茂盛的橡树，树上结满了猴子

ài chī de xiàng zǐ yú shì jū gōng duì mí hóu shuō nǐ men měi tiān fàn
爱吃的橡子。于是狙公对猕猴说："你们每天饭

hòu lìng wài zài chī yì xiē xiàng zǐ zǎo shang chī sān gè wǎn shang chī sì
后，另外再吃一些橡子。早上吃三个，晚上吃四

gè zěn me yàng
个，怎么样？"

hóu zi men tīng le fēi cháng shēng qì chǎo chǎo rāng rāng shuō tài
猴子们听了非常生气，吵吵嚷嚷说："太

shǎo le zěn me zǎo shang chī de hái méi yǒu wǎn shang duō jū gōng lián
少了！怎么早上吃的还没有晚上多？"狙公连

máng shuō nà me měi tiān zǎo shang chī sì kē wǎn shang chī sān kē zěn
忙说："那么每天早上吃四颗，晚上吃三颗，怎

me yàng hóu zi men tīng le dōu shí fēn gāo xìng jué de zǎo shang chī de
么样？"猴子们听了，都十分高兴，觉得早上吃的

bǐ wǎn shang duō le lù chū fēi cháng mǎn yì de shén qíng
比晚上多了，露出非常满意的神情。

During the Spring and Autumn period，in the State of Song there was once a man named Ju who kept many monkeys as pets. After living together with the monkeys for a long time，the man was familiar with their living style and the monkeys could understand his words.

There were too many monkeys and they needed much food

every day, but the man wasn't rich enough. So he decided to restrain their food. Nearby his house, there stood a tall oak tree laden with monkeys' favorite acorns. So the man said to the monkeys, "Every day after your meal, you can have some acorns. How about three in the morning and four in the evening?"

When the monkeys heard this, they looked very unhappy. They shouted, "Not enough. Why are we getting less acorns in the evening?" The man hurried to answer, "Then how about four in the morning and three in the evening?" The monkeys were very glad and satisfied that they could eat more in the morning than in the evening.

故事寓意 | The moral of the story

　　"朝三暮四"原指玩弄手法欺骗人,告诫人们要注重实际,防止被花言巧语所蒙骗。后来习惯用来比喻常常变卦,反复无常。这个故事启示人们要立场鲜明,明确目标,勇往直前,不要变化无常。

　　"Three in the morning and four in the evening" is used to refer to the tricky ways to fool people. It warns us that we should pay attention to the reality and not be cheated by flowery and deceiving words. Later the idiom is used to describe those who are inconsistent and change ideas often. It teaches us that we should have a clear-cut stand and clear goals, and just keep moving forward without wavering and hesitation.

自相矛盾

Self-contradiction

gǔ shí hou chǔ guó yǒu gè rén zài jí shì shang jì mài dùn yòu mài
古时候，楚国有个人，在集市上既卖盾又卖

máo shēng yi hěn qīng dàn wèi le zhāo lái gù kè shǐ dōng xi jǐn kuài mài
矛，生意很清淡。为了招徕顾客，使东西尽快卖

chū qù tā dà shēng jiào mài qǐ lái
出去，他大声叫卖起来。

tā shǒu xiān jǔ qǐ le shǒu zhōng de dùn xiàng zhe guò wǎng de xíng rén
他首先举起了手中的盾向着过往的行人

chuī xū dào dà jiā hǎo dōu lái kàn kan wǒ zhè kuài dùn pái zhè shì yòng
吹嘘道："大家好！都来看看我这块盾牌。这是用

zuì hǎo de cái liào duàn zào chéng de hǎo dùn ya zhì dì tè bié jiān gù rèn
最好的材料锻造成的好盾呀，质地特别坚固，任

píng nín yòng shén me fēng lì de máo yě bù kě néng chuō chuān tā yì fān
凭您用什么锋利的矛也不可能戳穿它！"一番

huà shuō de rén men fēn fēn wéi lǒng lái zǎi xì guān kàn
话说得人们纷纷围拢来，仔细观看。

接着，这个楚人又拿起了矛，不停地夸赞道：

"大家再看看我的这根长矛，它是我精心打制出来的好矛呀。矛头特别锋利，不论您用如何坚固的盾来抵挡，也会被我的矛戳穿！"他话刚讲完，在场的听众都十分诧异。

过了一会儿，只见人群中站出来一个男子，指着那位楚人问道："你刚才说，你的盾坚固无比，无论什么矛都不能戳穿；而你的矛又十分锋利，无论什么盾都不可抵挡。那么请问：如果我用你的矛来戳你的盾，结果会怎么样呢？"

那个楚国人听了，半天说不出话来。他只好涨红着脸，赶紧收拾好矛和盾，灰溜溜地逃离了集市。

In ancient times, a man of the State of Chu sold a spear and a shield in the market. In order to attract customers, he loudly boasted about them.

Holding the shield, he yelled to passersby, "Hello, everybody. Come and see my shield. It is a solid one made of the best material. Not even the sharpest spear can penetrate it." A large crowd were attracted to watch him and the shield.

Then the man held his spear and boasted, "Look at my spear. I made it with utmost care and its head is extremely sharp. No matter how solid your shield is, it could penetrate it." The audience were all puzzled.

Then a guy stepped ahead and asked, "You say that your spear is sharp enough to penetrate anything and your shield is solid enough for any attack. What would happen if your spear is used to pierce your shield?"

The man from Chu flushed and didn't know how to respond. He grabbed his spear and shield and left in dejection.

故事寓意 | The moral of the story

"自相矛盾"的意思是用自己的长矛刺自己的盾牌,用来比喻自己的言行相互抵触。这个故事告诉我们:说话、做事,不能前后矛盾,走极端,要注意分寸,并且留有余地。

"Self-contradiction" means using your spear to pierce your shield. This could be interpreted as contradict yourself in words and deeds. The story tells us that no matter what we say and do, we can't contradict ourselves or go to extremes. We should act properly and leave space for unforeseen circumstances.

后　记

　　中国古代寓言的发展源远流长，上可追溯至春秋战国，下可延续至唐宋元明清时期。这期间涌现的大量的优秀寓言作品，成为我国古典文学长河中的重要一脉。这些寓言故事展现了广大劳动人民纯厚、朴实的思想，闪耀着人民无穷的智慧和高尚的道德光芒。作品往往借用简洁易懂的故事来揭示深刻的道理，运用比喻、象征或拟人等精湛的艺术表现手法，巧妙地点示某种哲理，或讽刺，或启发，或劝诫，使读者能够从中受到感染，收获新知，得到启迪。尤为可贵的是，这些故事的主题和经验教训具有普适性的借鉴意义和参考价值，可以对不同国界、不同文化的读者在为人处世、生活学习等方面给予启示。

　　我国寓言博大精深，是中国传统文化中的重要内容，某种程度上对形塑伟大的中华民族精神和中国形象具有举足轻重的作用。作为一名教授和研究中国文学和文化的教师，我深深地感受到承担文化传承与创新的历史责任和使命。因此，聚焦中国传统文化，挖掘传统文化中最有价值、最具普适性精神内涵的精品，成为我思考和从事华文教育教学工作和研究的一个重要维度。因为重现和阅读它们得到的不仅是语言，或是美学上的享受，我们更能从中对中华文化、中国形象有更为深刻的认识。

在书稿即将付梓之时，在此，我向一直关心和支持我的领导、师长、亲友深表感谢。衷心感谢学校、学院各级领导、同事们的关心与支持，他们为我提供较好的科研平台，使我能够安心工作与著述，使本书能够顺利出版。衷心感谢浙江大学出版社的包灵灵女士、宋旭华先生等人，对本书做了精心指点，提出了宝贵的建议；衷心感谢泰国宋卡王子大学的林桃源、陈美琳、温玛丽、蔡青青、萧丽华、明明等 34 名同学，她们对我设计的关于文学经典鉴赏、汉语学习认知的调研工作不辞繁难地积极参与、乐在其中；感谢刘金程先生等人谋划、绘制了本书插图；我校汉语国际教育专业的学生施育恒、石政、刘林搜集、整理了相关资料，陈玉、崔艳萍对文稿做了校对工作，在此一并感谢。

我还要衷心感谢我的父母、哥嫂、其他亲人，他们宅心仁厚、安分守己和勤勉耐苦的美德，深深地影响并成就了我。同时，我还要感谢我的爱人和我刚满两周岁的小宝贝。有爱才有家，有家才有梦，有梦才能走更远。感谢所有亲友的一路陪伴，他们的不离不弃，使我克服一个个难题，坚持不懈地努力与前行。

　　本书选取的这些寓言故事，基本上是流传久远、普通老百姓耳熟能详的经典故事。我们希望这些故事能重述给不同国界、不同文化、各个年龄段的读者。由于时间仓促，难免会有疏漏和错误之处，敬请各位专家、学者不吝批评指正。希望在未来听取各方面的意见后，能有机会对本书加以修订。

李火秀

2016 年 2 月 8 日于赣州

Postscript

The development of Chinse ancient fables has experienced a long history, tracing back to the Spring and Autumn period and the Warring States period, and extending to the dynasties of Tang, Song, Yuan, Ming and Qing. During this period, large quantities of excellent fables were created and they became an important branch in the classical literature history of China. These fables illustrate the pure and sincere ideas of the working people and demonstrate the infinite wisdom and noble morality of Chinese people. In those fables, profound truths are often exposed through simple and easily comprehensible stories, and rhetorical features such as metaphor, symbolism and personification are used ingeniously to reveal a certain philosophy. They satirize, inspire or exhort, enabling readers to get enlightened and gain new knowledge. What is particularly precious is that the themes and messages of these stories are instructive and valuable universally, which would enlighten readers from different countries and civilizations in terms of life and work.

Chinese fables, broad and profound, are important components of traditional Chinese culture, and actually to a great extent they help to shape our national spirits and Chinese image. As a teacher that teaches and explores Chinese literature and culture, I could sense my responsibility and mission to inherit and innovate Chinese culture. Therefore, focusing on traditional Chinese culture and exploring the most valuable and universally instructive spirit have become a vital aspect of my research and teaching of Chinese language and culture. We can not only get linguistic or aesthetic enjoyment from reproducing and reading fables, but also have a deeper understanding of Chinese culture and image.

Now the book is going to be published, and I want to extend sincere gratitude to my dear leaders, teachers and friends who have been supporting me all the time. I would like to thank leaders and colleagues in my university and college for their help and care in providing me with such a good research platform which enables me to focus on my book and get it published. Heartfelt thanks also go to Ms. Bao Lingling and Mr. Song Xuhua from Zhejiang University Press for their meticulous guidance and valuable suggestions. I'm grateful to the 34 students from Prince of Songkla University in Thailand: Lin Taoyuan, Chen Meilin, Wen Mali, Cai Qingqing, Xiao Lihua, Ming Ming and so on, for their cooperation in my survey on literature classic appreciation and Chinese learning cognition. Thanks go to Liu Jincheng for drawing illustrations for this book and Shi Yuheng, Shi Zheng, Liu

Lin, students of our program of Teaching Chinese to Speakers of Other Languages, for doing me great favors in collecting and sorting documents. Gratitude goes to Chen Yu and Cui Yangping, students of our program, for their proofreading of this book.

I also want to thank my parents, brother and sister-in-law, and other relatives because their kindness and diligence have influenced and made me who I am. I also want to show my gratitude to my husband and my two-year-old baby daughter. Where there is love, there is home. A lovely home stimulates one to dream and achieve it. Thanks go to all the relatives and friends for their companion which helps me overcome challenges one by one and keep moving forward.

Most of the fables selected in this book are the best-known classic stories which are familiar to common Chinese people. We hope that these stories can be told to readers from different nations, with different cultures and in different ages. Due to the time rush, there may be many careless omissions and errors, and we sincerely expect that experts and scholars would leave their advice. We hope that in the future there is chance for us to revise this book after receiving comments and advice.

Li Huoxiu

February 8th, 2016, Ganzhou

图书在版编目(CIP)数据

中国经典寓言故事：英汉对照/ 李火秀，柯明星编
著.—杭州：浙江大学出版社，2016.9(2018.10 重印)
ISBN 978-7-308-16070-4

Ⅰ.①中… Ⅱ.①李…②柯… Ⅲ.①英语—汉语—
对照读物②寓言—作品集—中国 Ⅳ.①H319.4：I

中国版本图书馆 CIP 数据核字（2016）第 173397 号

中国经典寓言故事：英汉对照

李火秀　柯明星　编著

责任编辑	包灵灵
责任校对	董　唯
封面设计	杭州林智广告有限公司
出版发行	浙江大学出版社
	（杭州市天目山路 148 号　邮政编码 310007）
	（网址：http://www.zjupress.com）
排　　版	杭州林智广告有限公司
印　　刷	浙江新华数码印务有限公司
开　　本	889mm×1194mm　1/32
印　　张	8.25
字　　数	229 千
版 印 次	2016 年 9 月第 1 版　2018 年 10 月第 2 次印刷
书　　号	ISBN 978-7-308-16070-4
定　　价	35.00 元